TRAGIC KNOWLEDGE

TRAGIC KNOWLEDGE

Yeats's *Autobiography*
and Hermeneutics

DANIEL T. O'HARA

Columbia University Press
New York, 1981

Library of Congress Cataloging in Publication Data

O'Hara, Daniel T   1948-
  Tragic knowledge.

  Includes bibliographical references and index.
  1. Yeats, William Butler, 1865–1939. Autobio-
graphies. 2. Autobiography. 3. Hermeneutics.
I. Title.
PR5906.A532037   821'.8 [B]   80-26825
ISBN 0-231-05204-9

Columbia University Press
New York   Guildford, Surrey

For Joanne and Jessica Lynn O'Hara

Contents

Acknowledgments   ix

Introduction   1

1:   Self-Born Mockery: The 'Play'
       of 'Self'-Reflection in Yeats   7

2:   The Prospects of Memory   53

3:   The Genius of Technique   81

4:   The Faltering Image   115

Notes   163

Index   189

Acknowledgments

I WISH TO THANK Professors George Stade and A. Walton Litz of Columbia and Princeton Universities for their generous support of this project at a late stage in its development.

I also wish to thank Professor William V. Spanos of SUNY/Binghamton, editor of *Boundary 2: A Journal of Postmodern Literature,* for his help and his kind permission to reprint portions of "The Irony of Tradition and W. B. Yeats's *Autobiography*: An Essay in Dialectical Hermeneutics", (Spring 1977), 5: 679–710, which appear in revised form in chapters 1 and 4 of this study.

Professors Jonathan Arac and Paul Bové of the University of Illinois at Chicago Circle and the University of Pittsburgh have contributed greatly to my understanding of the contemporary critical scene. What light my work sheds on that is, therefore, a shared light.

As for Yeats and for my understanding of the ethics of reading poetry carefully, I owe more than I can estimate to Professor Taffy Martin of Emory University and to the poet Thomas Kinsella of Temple University.

To Professor Alan Wilde, also of Temple, to my parents, Daniel J. and Anna M. O'Hara, and to my wife, Joanne, I offer Nietzsche's highest praise: each in your own way is a "creator."

Finally: quotations from Yeats's *Autobiography* are reprinted with permission of Macmillan Publishing Co., Inc., copyright © 1916, 1935 by Macmillan Publishing Co., Inc., renewed 1944, 1963 by Bertha Georgie Yeats. Quotations from Yeats's *Collected Poems* are reprinted with permission of Macmillan Publishing Co., Inc. copyright © 1918, 1933 by Macmillan Publishing Co., Inc., renewed by Bertha Georgie Yeats 1940, 1946, 1961, 1968 by Bertha Georgie Yeats, Michael Butler Yeats, and Anne Yeats.

TRAGIC KNOWLEDGE

How few living men have a right to life
as against the mighty dead . . .
And if they are born late, there is a way
of living by which they can forget it . . . :
the knowledge that every "first nature"
was once a second and that every conquering
"second nature" becomes a first . . .
[so] future generations will know them only
as the first comers.

—Nietzsche, "Of the Use
and Disadvantage
of History For Life"

Introduction

AT THE OPENING of his autobiography, *Dichtung und Wahreit*, Goethe juxtaposes a prefatory letter from a friend that requests him to explain the connections that certainly must exist among his many great works, with the account of an incident from early childhood that tells how the budding genius once broke every piece of his mother's finest crockery before an appreciative audience of older neighborhood boys who cried out insistently after each scene of destruction for the future creator of *Faust* to produce "more, more!" How a reader, following the author's lead, makes something significant of such an ironic juxtaposition is, most generally, the subject of this study. More particularly, it is how ironic juxtapositions of this kind silently generate, even as they punctuate, the narrative structure of self-creation in autobiography. The idea of "tragic knowledge"—that, for both author and reader, such invisible nodes of irony produce as much as they reflect intense moments of unique self-consciousness—is, thanks to Nietzsche's insight into the process of textual indeterminacy and Ricoeur's dialectical method for understanding it, the way I make something of significance out of the irony that informs Yeats's *Autobiography*. The object of my study, then, is how, in one recent theorist's sly phrase, the "shifting blank"[1] at the center of such ironic juxtapositions receives a local habitation and a sublime name, however impersonal and daimonic the overtones, in this much-used but less-read text.

Of all the interpretive models currently available for treating this topic, I have found Paul Ricoeur's dialectical hermeneutics most appropriate for reading in a coherent and open-ended fashion the interplay of ironic juxtaposition and narrative elaboration present in a highly self-conscious text like Yeats's *Autobiography*. This is because Ricoeur's method is not polemical at all. Rather it is carefully dialectical, consisting in a first phase of demystifying critical analysis in the genealogical style of Nietzsche, Freud, and Heidegger; and a second phase of creative recuperation in the tradition of Hegel, Jung, and Eliade. The provisional "synthesis" of these two interpretive moments occurs only in the interpreter's wager of meaning—in his imaginative restoration of each individual text's unique "surplus" of meaning-potential.[2] Such a methodology, admittedly still rudimentary here, can perhaps, be a way, when fully developed, of answering Harold Bloom's antithetical critique of interpretation. For Bloom "only the agon is of the essence" in the reading encounter,[3] since he psychologizes the relation between author and critic into a literal power struggle for authority over the meaning of the text. But for Ricoeur, as we shall see in some detail later, this psychologistic formulation of the interpretive act represents only one moment in the impersonal dialectic of textual (self-)creation. Like the irony that pervades such a text as Yeats's *Autobiography*, Ricoeur's dialectic mediates between rather than simply cancels out the various possibilities of understanding that self one is always still becoming *like*. This hermeneutic irony produces a tragic (self-) knowledge of the limits of one's power to become autonomous.

Tragic Knowledge consists of two major phases: the outlines of a hermeneutic theory of how irony is represented in modern autobiographical texts, and the example of practical criticism—a detailed reading of one such text, Yeats's *Autobiography*. The first phase (chapter 1) traces the 'play' of 'self'-reflection as it appears in Yeats's particular case, in order to place the resulting work in the problematic context of autobiographical writing generally. This long first chapter begins with the generic question: what kind of consciousness is generated by the irony of textual indeterminacy as found in the autobiographical form? It then turns to the specifics of Yeats's situation (or "world") during his mid-life crisis of identity (the period immediately following the first collected edition of his work in the early years of the century). In doing so, I hope to work out the larger theoretical significance of his *Autobiography* both for the genre and for contemporary hermeneutics. The second, and by far the most extensive phase (chapters 2 to 4) descends repeatedly the dialectical ladder of interpretation within each chapter, from the implications of the theory presented in chapter 1 to the particulars of Yeats's text, only to reascend it again at the conclusion of each chapter to progressively larger questions. The justification for this method of tracing the hermeneutic circle is that in this way I test out (rather than simply exhaust) Ricoeur's paradigm of reading as presented in the first chapter.[4] In *Tragic Knowledge* I am attempting to incorporate both phenomenological description and critical interpretation within an open-ended dialectical hermeneutic of imaginative restoration. By enacting this dialectic in my text, I hope to give a temporal reading of Yeats's *Autobiography* rather than perform a New Critical operation upon its "spatial form" from the ideal and often falsifying perspective of the end.[5] After all, one of the pleasures of reading Yeats's *Autobiography* is seeing him gradually and ever so unexpectedly discover over many years of periodic composition (1908–1938), his original love of fate, his "radical innocence," so compatible with Nietzsche's own smiling Dionysian wisdom: "Accepting one self as if fated, not wishing one's self different—that is . . . *great reason* itself."[6]

Tragic Knowledge, then, may be seen as a double-edged project: it attempts to establish a theory of how irony is in-

3

terpreted in autobiographical writing, a theory which requires the development of a temporal, phenomenological
hermeneutics of autobiographical texts, a method of reading
which may have some significance as a possible model for
interpreting other kinds of texts, especially critical texts; and
it attempts to show how such a theory and such a method
combine to disclose the way in which Yeats's *Autobiography*
traces its author's "self-overcoming." For by means of an
increasingly self-critical irony, Yeats overcomes, first of all,
the burden of being influenced by so many different and
fragmentary lives (seen as "texts"), only to find that way of
reading others informing as well his own projected script,
when he seeks to revise his life of antithetical quest as one
of the "last Romantics" into a moral exemplum illustrating
the supposed virtues of the Anglo-Irish Ascendency. Yeats
finds that to be fully himself he must falter in his attempt to
become the poet of a dying class.

In light of this ironic development one could describe
the movement of Yeats's *Autobiography* from *Reveries* through
the *Trembling of the Veil* to *Dramatis Personae*, *Estrangement*,
and the rest in terms of Zarathustra's first parable to the
people of the town called "the Motley Cow." First, as I argue
in chapter 2 ("The Prospects of Memory"), Yeats must confront the burden of the past and become like a camel learning
to bear that burden, by becoming the ironic genealogist of
his own fragmentation and anxiety, tracing every recalcitrant
image back to its source in his earliest experiences. Then, as
I trace in chapter 3 ("The Genius of Technique"), Yeats must
become like a lion, and fiercely reconstruct the pattern of his
life and that of his friends' lives, thereby disclosing the
sources of his growing freedom in early manhood and middle
life as the times generally grow even worse. Finally, I contend
in the last chapter ("The Faltering Image") that, despite his
desire to idealize the bankrupt Ascendency culture as a still
living, creative force, Yeats must become like a child again

4

by allowing the irony of his tradition of texts (assembled as *The Autobiography* by him shortly before his death) to deconstruct and reconstitute the last traces of the Romantic image of the poet. In the end *The Autobiography* portrays Yeats as the foolish fond old creator who joyfully affirms life by desiring to come "Proud, open-eyed and laughing to the tomb,"[7] since he knows that only by accepting his tragic fate nobly as a member of a dying culture might he continue to sing amid his uncertainty, the artist playing with all the masks.

Some day setting out to find knowledge, like some pilgrim to the Holy Land, he will become the most romantic of characters. He will play with all masks. . . . We confess to Life and tell it all that we would do if we were young, beautiful and rich, and Life answers, "I would never have thought of all that for myself, I have so little time." And it is our praise that it goes upon its way with shining eyes forgetting us.[8]

The daimonic form of irony found in Yeats's *Autobiography* is then much like that which explodes the carefully wrought conclusion of Socrates' argument in *The Symposium*. When the drunken intrusion of Alcibiades and his company turns dialectical vision into Dionysian revels, everyone, including Socrates himself finally, is inclined no longer to speak of Eros in those figures which disclose even the greatest mind drawing a complete blank at times, but to begin to act in one way or another. Yeats's Nietzschean interpretation of the ironic moments of tragic knowledge defines the shape and thrust of the imaginative writer's career in a similarly "self-creative" style, one that has been made available once again, especially for this contemporary student of modernist literature, by Paul Ricoeur.

1

Self-Born Mockery: The 'Play' of 'Self'-Reflection in Yeats

"He who climbs upon the highest mountains
laughs at all tragedies, real or imaginary!"
—Nietzsche, "Of Reading and Writing,"

Thus Spoke Zarathustra

The Problem of Autobiographical Interpretation

An 1885 entry in Nietzsche's *Will to Power* profiles succinctly the problematic form of modern autobiographical reflection:

> *On German Pessimism*
> The eclipse, the pessimistic coloring, comes necessarily in the wake of the Enlightenment. Around 1770 the decline of cheerfulness began to be noticed; women, with that feminine instinct which always sides with virtue, supposed that immorality was the cause. Galiani hit the nail on the head. He cites Voltaire's verse:
>
> > *Un monstre gai vaut mieux*
> > *Qu'un sentimental ennuyeux.*
>
> When I believe that I am a few centuries ahead in Enlightenment not only of Voltaire but even of Galiani, who was far profounder—how far must I have got in the increase of darkness! And this is

7

really the case, and I bewared in time, with some sort of regret, of the German and Christian narrowness and inconsequence of pessimism *à la* Schopenhauer or, worse, Leopardi, and sought out the most quintessential forms (Asia). But in order to endure this type of extreme pessimism (it can be perceived here and there in my *Birth of Tragedy*) and to live alone "without God and morality," I had to invent a counterpart for myself. Perhaps I know why man alone laughs: he alone suffers so deeply that he *had* to invent laughter. The unhappiest and most melancholy animal is, as fitting, the most cheerful.[1]

Nietzsche deploys here an ironic historical perspective (the Enlightenment beginning and its decadent Romantic aftermath) on a significant issue of his day (the question of German Pessimism). He does so in order to chart in the text the emergence of his own eccentric sublimity (how the idea of his Dionysian counterpart, Zarathustra, overtook him).[2] All this is done in terms of an antithetical design of previous and still possible influences (Galiani, Voltaire, Schopenhauer, and even Leopardi), which only serves to highlight his own Promethean difference from his dangerously belated time (as seen in the growing chiaroscuro effect signaling the increase in him of both masculine Enlightenment and feminine pessimism). The result of this solitary creative act of self-reflection is that Nietzsche discloses to himself the tragic nature of man's laughter (its awful necessity) and its daimonic power of (self-)invention ("*Un gai monstre*," etc.). He thereby overcomes in himself his Romantic heritage. The ironic use of history to reduce the pretensions of the contemporary scene, the coercive imposition of a sublime antithetical design on that abbreviated slice of history, so as to recreate past origins in the interests of future aims—all represented as one's rediscovery of man's archetypal imagination: these are the three phases—the 'play'—of modern 'self'-reflection.

What is problematic about all this, of course, is that this

threefold process of ironic reduction, sublime recreation, and daimonic rediscovery bears a striking resemblance to the dialectic of revisionism, the poetics of misreading—"limitation," "substitution," "representation"—that Harold Bloom has identified as the essential pattern of post-Enlightenment literature.[3] The question for the reader of autobiography— that seemingly most mimetic and expressive of literary genres—now becomes: what is the relationship in autobiographical texts between the referential and reflexive dimensions of self-reflection, between what Roy Pascal has seen as autobiography's imaginative design and its truthful intention.[4]

A failure to address this question directly undermines even the most systematic theoretical positions on the genre and leads indirectly to the failures of practical critics when they attempt to read the more complex modern examples, as can be seen from the interpretations of Yeats's *Autobiography*.[5] A genuinely dialectical understanding of interpretation, of the dynamic inter-relationship of reference and self-reference, of description and redescription, such as is found in Paul Ricoeur's recent work, can provide the basis for a new theory of reading especially applicable to autobiographical reflection, one that can help to elucidate the creative hermeneutics of one of the most misunderstood modern instances, that composed over nearly thirty years by "the greatest poet to write English in our time."[6]

Currently, the most influential notions of autobiography are those defined by M. H. Abrams in *Natural Supernaturalism* (1971) and Paul de Man in *Allegories of Reading* (1979). According to Abrams, modern autobiographical reflection conforms to a genetic pattern of history best illustrated by Wordsworth's *Prelude* and Hegel's *Phenomenology of Mind*. Autobiography demonstrates most clearly the systematic process of secularization of religious forms begun in the Enlightenment. It represents the individual's life in terms of an internalized quest, not for salvation, nor for erotic communion, but for creative significance. Autobiography traces this quest from the imagination's wondrous if hazardous birth, through its eccentric development and self-conscious passion, to its intermittent pangs of spiritual rebirth:

> Much of what distinguishes writers I call "Romantic" derives from the fact that they undertook, whatever their religious creed or lack of creed, to save traditional concepts, schemes, and values which had been based on the relation of the Creator to his creation and creatures, but to reformulate them within the prevailing two-term system of subject and object, ego and non-ego, the human mind or consciousness and its transaction with nature. . . . *The Prelude*, correspondingly, is ordered in three stages. There is a process of mental development which, although at times suspended, remains a continuum; this process is violently broken by a crisis of apathy and despair; but the mind then recovers an integrity which, despite admitted losses, is represented as a level higher than the initial unity, in that the mature mind possesses powers, together with an added range, depth, and sensitivity of awareness, which are the products of the critical experiences it has undergone.[7]

Just as people in ages of faith once turned to the confessional genre to discover the providential plan secretly at work in their lives, so post-Enlightenment writers, who increasingly found this option denied them by the leveling fragmentation of all traditional forms, resort to the autobiographical mode to determine if perhaps some imaginative pattern of meaning—of personal continuity at least, however baleful—can be discovered beneath the apparently meaningless contingencies of modern existence. Thus, Abrams sees modern autobiography of the crisis variety as describing a Romantic or dialectical spiral. A state of original wholeness gives way to a fall into self-division, which, in turn, is superceded by the return, on a "higher," more "knowing" level, to a state of integration. For Abrams, the "soul" of autobiography is the working out of this epistemological "plot": a tree blossoming from the seed at last.

Paul de Man systematically calls into question the privileged status of this conventional understanding of autobiographical reflection that supports so much of the scholarly historical approach to literature. He sees the Romantic spiral as a conceptual metaphor for a certain historical form of critical interpretation that paradoxically refuses to reflect on its own historical nature. For de Man, autobiographical texts ironically subvert, rather than blindly follow, a genetic pattern of narrative development, by embedding in the structure of their rhetorical figures a critical commentary on this pattern, an "allegory of reading" that explodes from within all pretense to aesthetic or thematic closure, even that self-consciously professed by the most rigorous of contemporary analyses:

Within the epistemological labyrinth of figural structures [in such a critical text], the recuperation of selfhood would be accomplished by the rigor with which the discourse deconstructs the very notion of the self. The originator of this discourse is then no longer the dupe of his own wishes; he is as far beyond pleasure and pain as he is beyond good and evil or, for that matter, beyond strength and weakness. His consciousness is neither happy nor unhappy, nor does he possess any power. He remains however a center of authority to the extent that the very destructiveness of his ascetic reading testifies to the validity of his interpretation. . . . But the discourse by which the figural structure of the self is asserted fails to escape from the categories it claims to deconstruct, and this remains true, of course, of any discourse which pretends to reinscribe in its turn the figure of this aporia. There can be no escape from the dialectical movement of the text. . . . This irony is no longer a trope but the undoing of the deconstructive allegory of all tropological cognitions, the systematic undoing, in other words, of understanding. As such, far from closing off the tropological system, irony enforces the repetition of its aberration.[8]

De Man's deconstructive labyrinth opposes at every turn Abram's Romantic spiral, and even itself. Where for Abrams

11

Hegel and Wordsworth represent the highest achievements of autobiographical form, for de Man it is Nietzsche and Rousseau who best tunnel out in their various texts unfathomable abysses beneath the path of the secular pilgrim. The fiery seed of eternity, to mix metaphors here, is apt to bloom into the hyperactive cybernetic machine.[9]

If de Man has undermined the authority of Abrams' view, then this following recent comment of his undermines his own view as well: "nothing, whether deed, word, thought or text, ever happens in relation, positive or negative, to anything that precedes, follows or exists elsewhere, but only as a random event whose power, like the power of death, is due to the randomness of its occurrence."[10] Thus the Romantic Spiral and the Deconstructive Labyrinth appear as two perpetually recurring conceptual metaphors for the process of critical (mis-) understanding that constitutes literary history. Perhaps they are even two antithetical paradigms of interpretive activity that depend on each other as much as do the figures of father/son, master/slave, hero/victim. Both paradigms, at least as elaborated by Abrams and de Man, cover over the paradoxical generic intention of autobiographical reflection, which is to represent the truth of a life in symbolic form. Abrams, as we have seen, overlooks the question of the distorting nature of symbolic form, and de Man, as can be implied from his own silence on the matter, begs the question of the textual projection of truth by assuming, apparently from the outset, the purely deceptive essense of aesthetic representation. Whereas traditional scholar-critics like Abrams propound concepts that they intend to be univocal, stable, and pristine, contemporary theoreticians of deconstruction all too eagerly articulate sets of highly figurative terms that are just the self-conscious reverse: polyvalent, corrosive, and "explosive."

This is not to say that between them Abrams and de Man exhaust the possibilities of autobiographical theory or preempt the critical practice of interpreters of particular autobiographical texts. It would be too convenient to describe the diverse field of autobiographical study in terms of an ironic reversal, as if all contemporary critics of autobiography have simply turned Georg Misch's definition of the genre as "the description of a life written by the individual himself" around into its opposite, as Jeffrey Mehlman in fact has wittily done by claiming that autobiography is the textual inscription of "the impossibility of becoming alive to oneself" in the elusive realm of *écriture*.[11] To oppose Dilthey's historical hermeneutics to Derrida's deconstruction is too easy. As James Olney put it recently in his genial survey of the history of autobiographical criticism, both the genre and the reflections on it are too volatile and paradoxical to submit without protest to overly schematic categorizations: "what is autobiography to one person is history or philosophy, psychology or lyric poetry, sociology or metaphysics to another. . . . This is one of the paradoxes of the genre. Everyone knows what autobiography is, but no two observers, no matter how assured they are, are in agreement."[12] As if to support Olney's self-evident assertion, Michael Sprinker, in "Fictions of the Self: The End of Autobiography," even sees the critical act of interpretation as essentially autobiographical,[13] an insight made infamous by Oscar Wilde almost a century ago. Nevertheless, despite the proliferation of different definitions of autobiography and different approaches to particular examples of it—which range from the fragments of Heraclitus or the Enneads of Plotinus to Eliot's *Four Quartets*, Jung's psychology, Feminist tracts, Black Power polemics and everything in between—the definitive treatment of the special kind of self-consciousness generated in autobiographical reflections is Hegel's in *The Phenomenology of Mind*. In this, even Abrams and de Man would concur. That is why their work is theoretically significant. As Eugenio Donato and David Hoy have recently implied, those works which attempt to critique, to undo, or to evade Hegel in this regard, works such as Kierkegaard's *Repetition*, Heidegger's *Being and Time*, or Nietzsche's *Ecce Homo*, resurrect some portion of the very monument they would raze.[14]

Hegel's description of this unique autobiographical self-consciousness is intricate in both conception and expression. I quote at length with some trepidation:

In its act-of-going-inside-of-itself, Spirit is submerged in the night of its Self-Consciousness. But its empirical existence which had disappeared is preserved in this night. And this dialectically-overcome empirical-existence, that is, the existence which is already past, but which is engendered again from the Knowledge [of the past], is the new empirical-existence. It is a new historical World and a new concrete-form of Spirit. In the latter, Spirit must begin again in the immediacy of this form, and it must grow-and-ripen again starting with it; it must do so, therefore in just as naïve a manner as if everything that precedes were lost for it and it had learned nothing from the experience of earlier historical Spirits. But internalizing-Memory (*Er-Innerung*) has preserved this existence, and this Memory is the internal-or-private-entity, and in fact a sublimated (*hohere*) form of substance. Therefore, if this Spirit, while seeming to start only with itself, begins its formative-education (*Bildung*) again from the start, at the same time it begins it at a higher (*hohern*) level.[15]

This is the Hegel of Abrams' circuitous journey or Romantic Spiral. Yet Hegel's position is never one-sidedly dialectical:

Of this Spirit, which has left the form of Substance behind, and enters existence in the shape of self-consciousness, we may say, therefore—if we wish to use terms drawn from the process of natural generation—that it has a real mother but a potential or implicit father. For actual reality, or self-consciousness, and implicit being in the sense of Substance are its two moments; and by the reciprocity of their kenosis, each relinquishing or "emptying" itself of

14

itself and becoming the other, Spirit thus comes into existence as their unity.[16]

What Hegel is saying, in effect, is that "nature" ("a real mother") and culture ("a potential or implicit father") can at every point become one. That is to say, the genetic pattern of historical interpretation (The Romantic Spiral) and the ironic subversion of this pattern (The Deconstructive Labyrinth) constitute "a spiral labyrinth" in which the recollecting self pursues the traces of earlier wanderings in the hope of transforming the minotaur into Ariadne. The moment of interpretation becomes the eccentric measure of eternity.

Hegel presents his understanding of autobiographical reflection in clearer form in his interpretation of the death of Socrates from his *Lectures on the History of Philosophy*. For Hegel, when Socrates chooses death over either recantation or self-exile, he enacts the essential pattern of such self-conscious figuration of one's life:

In general history we find that this is the position of the heroes through whom a new world commences, and whose principle stands in contradiction to what has gone before and disintegrates it: they appear to be violently destroying the laws of that world. Hence individually they are justifiably vanquished, but it is only the individual, and not the principle, which is negated.[17]

Translated from the stage of world-historical irony to that of the individual life this means that at every turning point of that life a Socrates or a Christ in oneself must die if the principle, the point of view, the vision of that self is to live on to enable a new world to begin. To recall the opening example from Nietzsche: Voltaire and Galiani had once represented Nietzsche, they were his masks of Enlightenment before he had gotten so far ahead of them in both darkness and light, that is, before he could murder and recreate them in a text.

15

Hegel is so central to our understanding of the modern historical consciousness, the critical self-consciousness, embedded in autobiography because as Abrams points out in some detail Hegel has secularized salvation history into the autobiography of the Absolute Spirit as it wends its way on its circuitous journey from pure ignorance to absolute knowledge by recollecting as it goes along all the figures of its past life, whether this life is conceived as the collective progress of humanity or the development of the individual. In addition, Hegel has transformed the Neo-Platonic ladder of being into the sign-chain of interpretation, the stations on the way, that punctuate the narrative of man's development into god, a story that repeats in a speculative form the Christian mythos of the Passion, Death, and Resurrection of the God-Man. Thus for Hegel the natural pagan consciousness (or psyche) and the educated Christian self-consciousness (or logos) combine, as "real mother" and "implicit father," to produce the daimonic, Faustian spirit restlessly in pursuit of a state in which, to borrow Yeats's phrase, "passion is reality."[18] Rather than being the ultimate Baedeker for the ruins of time, Hegel's philosophy prophesies for our time as Augustine's did for another age the shape of things to come.[19]

Only a hermeneutics that comes to terms with Hegel's powerful historical myth and places it in a useful way within the current conflict of interpretations can hope to provide the basis for the development of a comprehensive practical criticism of autobiography that would resist the sterile eclecticism of recent theorists and would hold the promise, perhaps, of a more general theory of critical interpretation. But before attempting to show how Paul Ricoeur's hermeneutic phenomenology lays the foundations for such a new understanding of autobiography and of the interpretive act itself by allowing Ricoeur to guide my reading of Yeats's *Autobiography*, I want to examine in some detail the criticism

16

of and the backgrounds for that work, so as to highlight the need for this essay in dialectical hermeneutics.[20]

The Paradox of Yeats's Wilful Fire

Despite both Harold Bloom's vigorous assurance that Yeats's *Autobiography* represents the poet's "great achievement in prose"[21] and the fine demonstrations of the fact by a critical few—most notably, Joseph Ronsley, Ian Fletcher, and Marjorie Perloff[22]—the scholarly consensus on the topic, even among unconventional readers of Yeats, remains basically the same. Yeats's effort in the genre is "accidental" or "anecdotal" in design and "external" or "two-dimensional" in its portraits of others and, even more damningly, in its impressions of the creative life. For the majority of Yeats's critics, then, his autobiographical project is at best a discursive appendage to the main work, useful for explicating some of his more occasional poems or charting his own sense of the changes in his poetic style. In short, Yeats's *Autobiography* clearly does not deserve, let alone require, any attempt at extensive sophisticated explication in its own right.

For example, David Lynch in his recent book, *Yeats: The Poetics of the Self*, gives voice to the conventional wisdom—something of a paradox given his otherwise novel psychoanalytic approach to the poetry and drama[23]—when he asserts that Yeats's record of his own experiment in living is no work of genius, often seeming "unintended" and "incomplete."

He begins his *Autobiography* with *Reveries Over Childhood and Youth* in 1916 [sic]. The title sets the tone for the prose: it is a very beautiful, and appropriately poetic, series of impressions. But it is also an account, as Yeats's old friend George Russell (the mystic A. E., hardly the most practical of men) observed testily, of "pure externalities". . . . The other volumes are no better. . . . The man who

17

sat down to breakfast with Lady Gregory and dined with Wilde, Lionel Johnson, Arthur Symons, and J. M. Synge is not the intelligible phantasmagorical Poet; the story of the boy who did not become a grocer remains untold.[24]

Contrary to Lynch's common view, however, Yeats's *Autobiography* does not even try to tell "the *story* of the *boy* who did *not* become a *grocer*." Rather, it affirms the ironic life of the writer who would put into question, even to the point of tragic complication, the Romantic basis of all such narratives of facile opposition. For Yeats in his *Autobiography* becomes that "most romantic of all characters"[25]—the poet who begins a pilgrimage for self-knowledge, and ends up a broken if still unfinished man "playing with all the masks" (*A*, 318).

There are three reasons for the prevalence of the conventional view of Yeats's *Autobiography*. First of all, as Ronsley and Fletcher have shown in detail, one can read out of the *Autobiography* either one of two antithetical portraits of its creator. Ronsley, under Richard Ellmann's influence, sees Yeats as the representative modernist author, the maker of *A Vision*. Yeats is for him the last Romantic, who moves from imaginative innocence through the pains of experience to attain in the end a renewed innocence in a symbolic realm of his own design. Ronsley sees Yeats at the moment he arrives in Sweden to accept the Nobel Prize for literature as actually achieving Unity of Being.[26] Fletcher, on the other hand, perhaps thanks to Hugh Kenner's emphasis on the ironic nature of the poet's rhetoric,[27] sees a radically different Yeats. For Fletcher, Yeats is the habitually bitter, chronically alienated, and sublimely cynical old *poète maudit* (here Frank Kermode's influence looms large),[28] whose work falsely "mythologises" his past in the pursuit of the metaphysical comfort that infamous "artifice of eternity" can provide him. Yeats becomes for Fletcher, then, a man whose own grandiose aesthetic schematizations consistently backfire on him: they betray him for what he is by exposing the hollow nature of his idolatrous symbolic compensations.[29] Affected tragic eloquence is, after all, characteristic of more than one "pathetic aesthete."[30] Even the briefer studies by Perloff and James Olney that attempt to combine these two antithetical views—Perloff in a most interesting if purely pragmatic way that lacks theoretical sophistication and Olney by sacrificing the man's particular life to the Neo-Platonic Daimon's archetypal memory—do so in ways that overlook the complex generic pattern of interpretation that, regardless of the author's own aims, must inform any work of autobiographical reflection. As seen in both Hegel and Nietzsche, despite their significant differences, this pattern aims to reduce the present by taking an ironic historical overview on it and to recreate the past by reading a sublimely antithetical design into it, all so as to rediscover one's own representative creative potential. Naturally, the only appropriate response to such a spectacle, for the autobiographer himself, is the tragic smile of the incarnate daimon—either that of Christ or Dionysus, but certainly not that pallid smirk of the Neo-Platonic or gnostic seer.[31]

This apparent confusion among critics of the *Autobiography* that has been seen as confusion in the work brings us to our second reason. These same critics have also failed to make the most of background information about the origins of Yeats's need to write his own life and the long process of that life's composition (left, for all intents and purposes, ruinously incomplete). Consequently, they have failed to see how Yeats recognizes the need to avoid both the pitfalls of the Romantic spiral and the vortices of the deconstructive labyrinth—something that Ronsley and Fletcher, respectively, and in their individual idioms, do not manage to do. Perhaps Yeats in fact does so, as he suggests, by tracing his life in the *Autobiography* in the way the Creator, "who yawns in earthquake and thunder and other popular displays," certainly must toil "in rounding the delicate spiral of a shell—and also that of a question mark? (*A*, 187). In any event, it is to this background information that I must now turn.

Yeats's autobiographical project begins commonly enough with an identity crisis. For several years after the turn of the new century and due to personal and professional frustrations involving Maud Gonne (she marries Major McBride in 1903 while Yeats tours America) and the Abbey Theatre (the political scraps are interminable), Yeats begins to doubt his own imaginative powers. Chronically from now on he feels helpless to create "artistic order" (*A*, 251) out of the "bundles of fragments" (*A*, 128) that constitute his self and world. Possessing only possible imaginative orders and no necessary one, he finds that "the possible unities," the internalized and discredited traditional forms of representation, "seem without number" (*A*, 251). As a result, Yeats begins his *Journal* and so inaugurates the autobiographical project. He needs to keep "a record of his thoughts and feelings during this period of great strain in his personal and professional life."[32] That is, he needs to record his "experiment in living" for his own and posterity's sake. In a letter written to John Quinn as Yeats works on the "First Draft" of *The Trembling of the Veil* (1917), he announces that he hopes by writing his life to learn how to "lay the many ghosts" that still haunt and confuse him, to learn how to compose his own "style" of living that will be indistinguishable from the "moral radiance" of the tragic hero.[33]

Yeats's poem "Pardon Old Fathers" captures perfectly this motive for composing his life:

> Pardon, old fathers, if you still remain
> Somewhere in ear-shot for the story's end,
> Old Dublin merchant 'free of ten and four'
> Or trading out of Galway into Spain;

20

Old country scholar, Robert Emmet's friend,
A hundred-year-old memory to the poor;
Merchant and scholar who have left me blood
That has not passed through any huckster's loin,
Soldiers that gave, whatever die was cast:
A Butler or an Armstrong that withstood
Beside the brackish waters of the Boyne
James and his Irish when the Dutchman crossed;
Old merchant skipper that leaped overboard
After a ragged hat in Biscay Bay;
You most of all, silent and fierce old man,
Because the daily spectacle that stirred
My fancy, and set my boyish lips to say,
'Only the wasteful virtues earn the sun';
Pardon that for a barren passion's sake,
Although I have come close on forty-nine,
I have no child, I have nothing but a book,
Nothing but that to prove your blood and mine.
                                        January 1914[34]

With this masterful example of Ciceronism, Yeats hopes to counter Katharine Tynan's portrait of him as a dreamy aesthete and George Moore's ridicule of his family's bourgeois origins in their recent autobiographies. The mastery comes in admitting all: to being both a devotee of Art for Art's Sake and the scion of commercial traders. But in admitting all this Yeats makes a virtue of necessity by bestowing on his ancestors and even on himself in the very intensity of his "barren passion" a heroic glitter. That Yeats accomplishes this feat without either alienating his father with this aristocratic, Nietzschean pose the latter so detested or suppressing the truth, testifies to Yeats's ability to embody truth in his symbolic designs without really knowing it.[35]

But there is another aspect to this painful project of laying ghosts and purifying his imagination. Yeats provides an important perspective on his autobiographical project in passages from two essays, one written in 1904 and the other in 1908, both of which are entitled "First Principles." These pieces, although inspired by his theater work, bear decisively on the formation of his aesthetic goals generally, especially as they relate to the writing of his life. Yeats says in the first of these that if a poet's art "does not seem, when it comes down to it, to be the creation of a new personality, in a few years it will not seem to be alive at all." The poet's art must create this "new personality," this "mask," not to escape the old ego shaped by circumstance, but to explore and to reveal, so as to understand, that "something in our minds we had never known of had [the poet] never imagined." The poet must explore those possibilities of our imagination that can show us what we can become by dramatizing them in his creative work. By doing so, he provides us with a perspective on what we must choose to become. The poet's mind is for Yeats as it was for Shelley a microcosm of the macrocosmic human mind, which is generated by the texts of the folk and of those "unacknowledged legislators," the poets.[36]

Yeats clarifies this idea in a passage from the "First Principles" written in 1908. Here he compares scientists, who in their naming and analyzing of the external world are like "new Adams," with artists, who are "Adams of a different Eden." He extends the comparison in an important way:

Artists are Adams of a different Eden, a more terrible Eden, perhaps, for we must name and number the passions and motives of men. There, too, everything must be known, everything understood, everything expressed; there, also, there is nothing common, nothing unclean; every motive must be followed through all the obscure mystery of its logic. Mankind must be seen and understood in every possible circumstance, in every conceivable situation.

Yeats makes it clear that this aesthetic ideal is not isolated

22

from a moral concern. He goes on to add that

There is no laughter too bitter, no irony too harsh for utterance, no passion too terrible to be set before the minds of men. The Greeks knew that. Only in this way can mankind be understood, only when we have put ourselves in all the possible positions of life, from the most miserable to those that are so lofty that we can only speak of them in symbols and in mysteries, will entire wisdom be possible.

Yeats concludes this rather Nietzschean paean by claiming that "upon this knowledge" "all wise government depends," and that, like the scientist, the artist rejoices "in battle, finding the sweetest of all music to be in the stroke of the sword."[37] Although this is not the place to examine at length Yeats's peculiar combination of Pater's aestheticism and Nietzsche's "gay science," it is clear that for Yeats the artist should become the heroic explorer of his own life and the ironic organizer of his own mind, so that, by transfiguring the possibilities found there into dramatic portrayals in his work, all of us may understand ourselves a little better: tragic knowledge with a vengeance.

This "experimental" metaphor for his autobiographical reflection—a metaphor that recalls the daimonic image of the speculative interpreter from Plato's *Symposium* (Socrates as Eros)[38]—brings us to the third and last reason why Yeats's critics have neglected to read this work carefully enough, namely, Yeats's irony. It manifests itself in the *Autobiography* in several basic ways: in the highly theatrical effects of its anecdotes as revealed by a comparison of initial and revised versions of key passages; in the incorporation in the text itself of a critical history of its own antithetical method of interpretation; and finally, in the explosion of its own carefully drawn designs.

Compare, for example, Yeats's original and revised formulas characterizing his relationship with George Russell (A.E.). At first Yeats portrays both Russell and himself as exemplary "life-praisers" who differ only in their methods of poetic composition: "I putting the legs of the compass before I draw my circle always nearer and nearer one another, and he always enlarging his interests."[39] But then, in final form, this difference so playfully appropriate for measuring the former art students, becomes all-important, critical. It becomes in fact the central synecdoche of a systematic opposition between two men, both of whom have been unfortunate enough to have been born into the wrong age. Russell becomes a stylized visionary decadent and Yeats a version of the heroic creator increasingly jealous of any threat to his own autonomy: as if he were "creation's very self" (*A*, 183). Russell appears now to be possessed by a dissolute imagination that cannot survive without the traditional religious and moral props all but completely denied him by his time: "I think Russell would not have disappointed even my hopes had he . . . met with some form of traditional belief" (*A*, 185). Yeats, on the other hand, needs here only the particulars of the poet's craft to check his wandering mind and compose— for brief moments at least—his own internal divisions into living imaginative orders. Russell, unlike Yeats, becomes a man wholly of his era: abstract, fragmented, rhetorical—another victim, like Wilde or Dowson, of genius in a bad time.

Not only does Yeats make the original difference in aesthetics the basis for the symbolic development of entire personalities which fundamentally oppose each other, but he also tears this revised explanation of Russell as *poète maudit* out of its original context (as he does some of his other explanations of his ruined friends). Chronology dictates that this passage on Russell appears at the beginning of "Ireland After Parnell." But in the final version of the *Autobiography* it appears near the conclusion of this section, inserted there as a symbolic bridge to the next part, "Hodos Chameliontos." Yeats thereby prepares us for his ultimate overcoming of the crises of vision that afflict Russell and his frantic, Hamlet-like disciples: he will achieve this "end" through the superior manipulative power of his intellect: "for it is only when the intellect has wrought the whole of life to drama, to crisis, that we may live for contemplation, and yet keep our intensity" (*A*, 183–84). Yeats lives through the crisis of identity by re-living and re-shaping the crises of his friends, each of whom, like Russell, becomes in the process representative of another of his own imaginative potentialities. Thus Yeats, like Nietzsche in my opening example or Joyce throughout his works, employs an antithetical method of self-interpretation, a psychomachia for concretizing error, learned (in Yeats's and Joyce's case) from Blake. He does so, not to disclose self and world but rather to coerce and enclose—so as to master—the images of both that he so anxiously wants to hand down to his readers: "We begin to live when we have conceived life as tragedy" (*A*, 128). Perhaps Yeats does become no more than a "pathetic aesthete" who affects tragic pose and eloquence as consolation for his self-fulfilling "prophecies"?

If, however, we examine this revision even more carefully and are willing to risk a sympathetic recovery of Yeats's text, we will see, I believe, that the conclusion of the revised passage actually belies and reverses such self-conscious and self-serving artifice—despite all appearances to the contrary—by ironically enacting it. As such, it overturns, by anticipating, our critical suspicions and deconstructions. For Yeats "ends" the revised version not, as might be expected, with the opening compass metaphor which marks the earlier version, but with an even grander symbol: "Is it not certain that the Creator yawns in earthquake and thunder and other popular displays [like nationalist riots or abortive visionary politics], but toils in rounding the delicate spiral of a shell?"

25

(*A*, 187). Yeats's common Pre-Raphaelite misreading of Blake's famous (and so-called) "Ancient of Days" engraving, which informs the original figure of the compass, has been transformed here into this most forbidding of images for the Creator, this most necessary archetype for the modernist poet to confront. For this involuted, "shell-like" rhetorical question self-consciously projects its own craftsman-like Deity for the artist in Yeats to emulate in his distancing of himself not so much from Russell as from that "potential Russell" who is still inscribed in the texts of memory and so still victimizes Yeats's creative self. Once made conscious and written down, Russell is no longer an anonymous competing voice for the creator to contend with. He becomes instead a figure of imaginative difference. Finally, and most crucially, it now becomes clear that in modern poetic autobiography the significant details recollected from the past are not literal at all, but are the ruling figures of earlier (self-)interpretations that haunt the mind; nor, for that matter, are these spectral injunctions so much distorted by revision as clarified and elaborated: ironically amplified. One's "life" is thus a critical history of possible models of selfhood for a *yawning* questionable Creator.

As if to reinforce this complex act of irony, Yeats's *Autobiography* is so imaginatively reflexive that it includes embedded in the play of its rhetorical structures a critical gloss on the method of its own generation of the Romantic plot of the genre. The passages on Macgregor Mathers' art of meditation offer the best instances. Mathers teaches the young Yeats that repeated meditation—to the point of exhausting the conscious will—upon the intricate and severe configurations of an abstract geometrical symbol (an antithetical mandala, if you will), can provoke into consciousness concrete images of a visionary intensity that, apparently springing from the Anima Mundi or the Great Memory conceived as a text, may suggest the necessary impersonal solution to one's otherwise insoluable, self-destructive personal dilemmas.[40] Such prefigurations of an imaginative resolution are as "unforeseen, as completely organized, as the images that pass before the mind between sleeping and waking" (*A*, 222). They assume final form only as they suddenly emerge into the conscious mind from the unconscious psyche, where they have been germinating anonymously for some time. It is as if Yeats's Anima Mundi were, in ironic fulfillment of the Arnoldean prophecy, the rich meta-text of sublime touchstones, those internalized cultural traditions initialled by and intialling in us the differential play of interpretations.

When Mathers first works his magic on Yeats, for example, the latter has recently returned to London's model Pre-Raphaelite Bedford Park section only to discover all his boyhood memories of and hopes for the area, its mystery and charm, shattered by the dissillusioning spectacle of leaky roofs, clogged drains, and complaint committees. He begins seriously to wonder then if his imagination can possibly survive the chronic state of transition which seemingly defines the entire modern world. But employing Mather's meditative art discloses for Yeats an image, constitutive of his creative self, of the fierce but wily patriarch of all wise imaginative survivors:[41]

> He gave me a geometrical cardboard symbol and I closed my eyes. Sight came slowly, there was not that sudden miracle as if the darkness had been cut with a knife . . . but there rose before me mental images that I could not control: a desert and a black Titan raising himself up by his two hands from the middle of a heap of ancient ruins. (*A*, 125)

Like the notorious drunken soldiery of "Byzantium," survivors of many cycles of creation and ruin, such consciously provoked images of the unconscious spontaneously compose themselves into a dramatic scene according to their own inherent phantasmagoric logic—one not dependent, it appears, on either mere association or previous suggestion. At the center of such elaborated or regenerated texts, Yeats hopes to witness, as if all creation's secrets suddenly come together and rise up before him, the slowly emerging realization of that "impersonal" or archetypal image of the creator—his "god-image"[42]—which he calls the "simplifying image," the "anti-self," or the "Daimon."[43]

What we see here in this passage on Mathers' meditative art is, then, Yeats's text in imaginative anticipation of its critic's reading of it. Repeatedly, over a considerable period of time Yeats (and his reader after him) imposes an abstract antithetical design of figures on the latent symbolic details that are embedded in memory's texts. Such texts are recollected according to this antithetical method because they concern the essential difference between his own and other people's imaginations. By making this difference conscious Yeats purges his imagination of his previously unconscious and potentially self-destructive identifications with others. Thus through a process of antithetical memory and defensive narration Yeats discovers his creative self and so discloses his only necessary world. In this complexly ironic way, he can overcome two of his extreme mental habits: both his tendency to rise ever higher into the expanding sphere of abstract antithetical generalization (A, 127), and his tendency to become, in simplistic reaction to the modern world helplessly immersed in the flux of imaginative and occult experience (A, 176, 181). Mathers' method, and Yeats's text, teach him to hesitate creatively between both extremes. As we shall see, the incorporation of these tendencies within a single dialectical interpretative method does not inspire claims to final synthesis but rather the "deferment" or subversion of all movement toward final syntheses.

But the most systematic form of irony—of a daimonic

nature—is that which can be found just about everywhere in the final text of Yeats's *Autobiography*, and which is the object of my reading throughout this study. From this point on, I will be relying a great deal less on the historical and biographical backgrounds to the text but only somewhat less on the intentional formal designs Yeats seeks to emobdy in it. On the whole, I will focus my analysis on the way irony develops repeatedly in the text from a defensive, metaphoric measure used to reduce the trivial present in light of a monumental past, to a symbolic method for recreating or staging one's life as a sublimely heroic drama, so as to recover one's lost imaginative power, which is represented in a mythic image of the daimonic creator. This figural representation of irony constitutes Yeats's famous quest for his "anti-self," for the Daimon who is his destiny. More will be said about this quest both later in this chapter (at least briefly) and in this study (at greater length). Suffice it to say for now that in this romance of interpretation one sees how Yeats figures the irony of all aesthetic representation as daimonic: "The Daimon, by using his mediatorial shades [which include the beloved] brings man again and again to the place of choice, heightening temptation that the choice may be as final as possible, imposing his own lucidity upon events, leading his victim to whatever among works not impossible is the most difficult."[44] In short, Yeats's relatives and friends, precursors and contemporaries, all function as the "mediatorial shades" or "masks" of the daimonic will at the center of the spiral labyrinth of textual representation. Representing the irony of aesthetic representation in a figure (the archetype of the Daimon) invites an indeterminate number of interpretive conceptions, all of which combine to avoid final synthesis, leaving a semantic void in the process of understanding the text, a seductive lacuna one never hesitates to penetrate with the god-mask of one's own choosing made in the image of all that one is not. Tragic knowledge is the awareness that this fateful self-transfiguration is an inescapable "autobiographical" moment in the hermeneutics of irony. The temptation of this situation is to construct a history of the genre based on how different practitioners and theorists of autobiography have figured irony in their texts.[45] But such temptation should be resisted, since, as we have seen, the two most systematic and authoritative attempts to define the genre, Abrams' Romantic Spiral and de Man's Deconstructive Labyrinth, are themselves complementary "readings" of the negative moment of irony in the Hegelian dialectic. And this, despite Abrams' careful scholarly distance and de Man's philosophical rigor. Only an explicitly dialectical hermeneutics, then, that confronts this strange fate of literary history, can hope to expose the operations of irony in autobiography without succumbing to the seductions of the very thing one wishes to examine critically.

When one does finally examine a passage from *The Autobiography* closely, one can see why most of its critics find it easier to overlook its complexities than to attempt to fathom them. Beginning to read the text seriously is like being lost on what Yeats calls "Hodos Chameliontos," the Path of the Chameleon, where image calls up image in a never-ending procession that can bewilder and debilitate even the most creative mind. Yet despite all this one of the more distinctive features of Yeats's mature prose is its curious tone of authority arising from amidst its notorious Pateresque effects. This puzzling mark of style can even be found when Yeats takes great pains to be starkly schematic and uncharacteristically laconic, as in the following passage from an early section of *Reveries*:

Two pictures come into my memory. I have climbed to the top of a tree by the edge of the playing field, and am looking at my schoolfellows and am proud of myself as a March cock when it crows to its first sunrise. I am saying to myself, "If when I grow up I am as clever among grown men as I am among these boys, I shall be a famous man." I remind myself how they think all the same things and cover the school walls at election time with the opinions their fathers find in the newspapers. I remind myself that I am an artist's son and must take some work as the whole end of life and not think as others do of becoming well off and living pleasantly. The other picture is of a hotel sitting-room in the Strand, where a man is hunched up over the fire. He is a cousin who has speculated with another cousin's money and has fled from Ireland in danger of arrest. My father has brought us to spend the evening with him, to distract him from the remorse that he must be suffering. (*A*, 26–27)

The passage is representative of the volume and of the entire autobiographical project in several ways. First of all, these "pictures" seem to irrupt ironically into Yeats's composed reflections, with little explicit referential or reflexive contextualization. The effect on the reader is rather like the abrupt emergence of a smouldering volcano on a tourist's horizon: purely mundane matters dwindle suddenly into insignificance. Second, the passage in itself can offer support for a suspicious view of Yeats's interpretive designs. Present intention appears so thoroughly to inform the recollection of past details (as manifested in both the reiteration of "I remind myself" and the self-conscious words of the young boy's sublime dedication to art), all in accord with an obvious antithetical pattern (*poète maudit* vs. bourgeois) that one could argue plausibly that as much distortion as disclosure of autobiographical truth is going on here. Third, there is an allusive aura surrounding each "picture" suggesting Romantic and more archetypal associations. The figure of the March cock and that of the criminal cousin reverberate with Wordsworthian and Byronic resonances, and the tree-climbing recalls the famous fruit-stealing incident from St. Augustine's *Confessions*—the latter another occasion of prideful rebellion against the ways of this world. The passage in this fashion

31

invites a kind of dialectical moralization, in which the opposition between the young boy's self-dedication to art and
his own cleverness is ironically represented in the cousin's
criminal speculation with another cousin's inheritance. That
is, an antithesis turns into a dialectical synthesis, into a cau-
tionary tale of how vain aspiration can become just another
conventional form of penitent self-exile. Finally, however,
based either on one's familiarity with Yeats's preference for
antithesis (for example, in *A Vision*) or his symbolic understanding of figurative language ("a flower in the wallpaper
may be an originating impulse to revolution or to philosophy"—*A*, 176),[46] the passage can be read as an experiment
in impressionistic prose illustrating the conflict between Art
and Life, or as a *symboliste* emblem demonstrating how the
purely formal properties of words, even in a highly referential genre, can produce a great array of possible meanings
or sets of meanings that playfully hover in the white spaces
of the text. In effect, Yeats's "external" text, so "accidental"
in its design, is apparently a fearful labyrinth, a wilful
paradox:

Who should be free if [the poet] were not? for none other has a
continual deliberate self-delighting happiness—style, "the only
thing that is immortal in literature," as Sainte-Beuve has said, a
still unexpended energy, after all that the argument or the story
need, a still unbroken pleasure after the immediate end has been
accomplished—and builds this up into a most personal and wilful
fire, transfiguring words and sounds and events. It is the playing
of strength when the day's work is done, a secret between a craftsman and his craft, and is so inseparate in his nature, that he has
it most of all amid overwhelming emotion, and in the face of death.
Shakespeare's persons, when the last darkness has gathered about
them, speak out of an ecstasy that is one half the self-surrender
of sorrow, and one half the last playing and mockery of the vic-
torious sword, before the defeated world. . . . It is in the arrangement of events as in the words, and in that touch of extravagance,

32

of irony, of surprise, which is set there after the desire of logic has been satisfied and all that is merely necessary established, and that leaves one, not in the circling necessity, but caught up into the freedom of self-delight.[47]

Before attempting to address this question, "Who should be free if [the poet] were not?," by giving my reading of the passage from Yeats's *Autobiography*, I want to interrupt my critical narrative and turn now to a consideration of Paul Ricoeur's hermeneutic phenomenology.

The Dialectical Hermeneutics of Paul Ricoeur

Paul Ricoeur cuts an uncertain figure in most avant-garde critical circles. Uncertain in the sense that, depending on the critic discussing, usually attacking him, Ricoeur appears as either an "unworldly" quietistic hermeneut or a "naïve" believer in the presence of the world as the reference point of a text.[48] This is not the place to engage in a full-scale defense of Ricoeur, nor am I necessarily the best person to mount such a defense.[49] What I would like to suggest to Ricoeur's literary-minded critics is that perhaps they misunderstand him: they have not followed the development of his philosophy, and so pick up one isolated statement here and another there and fail, quite understandably, to see him steadily and whole. Partisan polemics of one kind or another often obscure what is of use in a theorist, and Ricoeur himself, unfortunately, has at times given in to the temptation to make debater's points rather than to seek to elucidate the confusion he sees in an opponent's position.[50]

I would like to trace briefly the history of Ricoeur's development in order to place him within the proper context on the contemporary "post structuralist" scene, before focusing on one strand in that development, namely, his shift from a symbol-oriented Romanticist hermeneutics to a metaphor-centered, more "impersonal" kind of philosophical hermeneutics akin to Hans Georg-Gadamer's.

To anticipate somewhat: I find extremely useful Ricoeur's understanding of interpretion as an act in which the reader encounters the poet's creative or "excessive" redescription of reality, an encounter that enables the text "to give a Self to the ego."[51] What Yeats sees as the poet's tragic "freedom" or "irony," Ricoeur describes as that "surplus" of meaning-potential generated by living metaphor. I would contend that this description of the reader-text encounter is particularly applicable to modern autobiographical reflection, both in the case of the autobiographer himself and his critic. The irony of the textual production of the self, however painful or wounding a process—wounding to our primal narcissism—is interpreted by Yeats (among others) as a tragic form of knowledge constitutive of a transpersonal Self whose existence is a perpetual creation of the imagination daimonically (and not personalistically) conceived: "I think that all happiness depends on the energy to assume the mask of some other self; that all joyous or creative life is a re-birth as something not oneself, something which has no memory and is created in a moment and perpetually renewed" (A, 340). The interpretive act for both Ricoeur and Yeats, then, is an open-ended, dialectical predicament that transfigures the individual, in Yeats's terms, into a daimonic figure, one of our modern culture's exuberant "self-born mockers." Ricoeur's dialectical hermenoutics, in short, can provide both a sound basis for reading Yeats's creative hermeneutics of irony in The Autobiography and of understanding his exemplary tragic humanism in a way that can begin to answer Harold Bloom's "de-idealizing" and psychologizing critique of Yeats, in particular, and more generally, of the interpretive act itself. Ricoeur's dialectical hermeneutics, in other words, engage in a continuous dialogue with Hegel's speculative dialectic that is very useful for the purposes of literary study, a dialogue out of which emerges a position that resists both the urge for systems and the charms of nihilism.

In a 1971 essay, "From Existentialism to the Philosophy of Language," Paul Ricoeur reflects on the course of his career. He sees that course as a journey from his early existential phenomenology (derived from Husserl and Gabriel Marcel) with its emphasis on describing the structure of man's finite will, to a hermeneutic phenomenology (developed in his encounter with Freud and Lévi-Strauss), that recognizes the determining role played by language, its differential rules and formative codes, in the constitution of man's understanding of himself and his world.[52] Ricoeur at first simply takes for granted the language he uses to describe the will. But then, in *The Symbolism of Evil* (1962) and *Freud and Philosophy: An Essay on Interpretation* (1965), Ricoeur engages in an effort to develop a hermeneutics of the symbol that would not only account for the double-meaning intentionality of both religious and dream symbolism, but would also mediate between the recuperative hermeneutics of theology and the reductive hermeneutics of critical suspicion. At this time Ricoeur argues that the verbal symbol is a stratified linguistic structure in which the archaic phantasms of the unconscious prefigure the creative potentialities of reason, thanks to the mediating agency of cultural tradition. For example, Sophocles's *Oedipus Rex* builds a tragedy of the prideful *tyrannus* upon the originating complex of the pysche via the mythic and cultic narratives of the Greek people. In other words, the tragedy of the rational ruler undone by fate is founded on the tragedy of the family romance as sublimated by the legend of Oedipus, the cultural hero. The final "meaning" of the play, therefore, is neither that which an "archaeology of the subject" may reveal, nor that which a "teleology of the self" suggests; neither desire nor reason

35

alone forms the "meaning" of the play. Rather, that "meaning" is what the entire dialectic of figures, stretching from the phantasms of the Oedipal wish to the symbols of the hero, projects in the form of the drama itself: "My book on Freud, published in 1965, reflects this double recognition, first of the necessity of the detour through indirect signs, and secondly, of the conflictual structure of hermeneutics, and thus of self-knowledge. Self-knowledge is a striving for truth by means of this inner contest between reductive and recollective interpretations."[53] For Ricoeur, then, neither the "de-idealizing" critiques of structuralism and deconstruction, nor the recuperative understandings of traditional historical and formalist interpretations are satisfactory in isolation from or in blind contention with each other.

Ricoeur comments on this earlier attempt at constructing a "general hermeneutics" on the basis of symbolic language by noting the narrow scope of his definition of hermeneutics as the deciphering of double–meanings and its Romantic, specifically Hegelian, cast.[54] Ricoeur feels the inadequacy of this hermeneutics of the symbol so strongly due to the development in France of structuralism and the emergence in Germany of a theory of hermeneutics based on Heidegger's "destructive" phenomenology of the self. Ricoeur sees his task now as one of elaborating a hermeneutics that would focus on the "objective" structures of the text and would seek to explicate how these structures act on the reader to lead him to appropriate the meaning inscribed in the text as his own. The critique of mimesis and reference found in poststructuralist theories of interpretation must be answered, Ricoeur believes, rather than simply ignored or derided. Ricoeur replaces his dialectic of faith and suspicion with the dialectic of explanation and understanding, and shifts his attention from the hermeneutics of the symbol, which still depend largely on the communal acceptance of mythic narratives and religious beliefs, to the rule of metaphor in the discourse of philosophical speculation and critical analysis. As we will see, this shift in Ricoeur's position is a significant development, especially for the literary critic working on autobiography.

Ricoeur's position, then, is one that stands between structuralism and Heideggerian hermeneutics on the one hand, and the more traditional historical and formalist approaches on the other. Nevertheless, Ricoeur's most recent work does not simply break with his past concern with the structures of the will. Rather, he now sees those structures in terms of the problem of language, a problem that centers for him around the Christian proclamation of man's fallible if free will and God's providential if mysterious salvation plan:

What we need now is a new framework which would allow us to connect Biblical hermeneutics to general hermeneutics conceived as the question of what is understanding in relation to text-explanation. It is the function of general hermeneutics to answer problems such as: What is a text? i.e. what is the relation between spoken and written language? What is the relation between explanation and understanding within the encompassing act of reading? What is the relation between a structural analysis and an existential appropriation? Such are the general problems of hermeneutics to which a Biblical hermenutics has to be submitted.[55]

But for my purposes in this study there is no need to accept Ricoeur's religious orientation to find his theory of hermeneutics useful for characterizing in a philosophical manner the ways in which Yeats interprets that "excess" of meaning-potential of living metaphor that I term "irony." In fact, Ricoeur's most recent works, especially *Interpretation Theory: Discourse and the Surplus of Meaning* and *The Rule of Metaphor: Multi-disciplinary Studies of the Creation of Meaning in Language*, present highly suggestive arguments for the secular literary critic.[56]

Ricoeur's theory of language and interpretation is given

in definitive form in *Interpretation Theory*.[57] Here, he constructs a complex dialectic out of the antithesis of explanation and understanding. The impersonal, linguistic, and conventional features of a discourse and the personal appropriation of the unique event of meaning by the individual reader require a dialectical approach that applies the structuralist method of analysis to expand (rather than to explode) the moment of understanding. The act of interpretation must include a critical suspicion of all purely Romantic views of the text as the self-expression of an individual genius. A text does not, for Ricoeur, simply represent the world of its original audience, nor does it simply express the original intention of its author; and the interpreter must be on guard against these Romantic notions by adopting the "objectivist" strategy of structuralist analysis, especially as the latter has been applied to narrative. What the text does do is to inscribe and to transform by such inscription the original sense and reference via the mediating agency of discourse, its discipline of conventions, so that "a possible world" and "a possible way of being" in that world are both projected by the text as a series of metaphoric injunctions to be realized imaginatively by the careful reader:

What is indeed to be understood—and consequently appropriated—in a text? Not the intention of the author, which is supposed to be hidden behind the text; not the historical situation common to the author and his original readers; not the expectations or feelings of these original readers; not even their understanding of themselves as historical and cultural phenomena. What has to be appropriated is the meaning of the text itself, conceived in a dynamic way as the direction of thought opened up by the text. In other words, what has to be appropriated is nothing other than the power of disclosing a world that constitutes the reference of the text. In this way we are as far as possible from the Romanticist ideal of coinciding with a foreign psyche. If we may be said to coincide with anything, it is not the inner life of another ego, but the disclosure of a possible way of looking at things, which is the genuine referential power of the text. . . . In this sense, appropriation has nothing to do with any kind of person to person appeal. It is instead close to what Hans-Georg Gadamer calls a fusion of horizons (*Horizonverschmelzung*): the world horizon of the reader is fused with the world horizon of the writer. The ideality of the text is the mediating link in this process of horizon fusing.[58]

All that a writer desires to become and all that he desires his world to be combine with all that a reader desires to become and all that he desires his world to be in the dialectical act of interpretation. Or, as Yeats would say, "art is but a vision of reality" for the individual whose "passion is reality." With this kind of formulation, Ricoeur incorporates a post-structuralist perspective and the Heideggerian outlook of Gadamer into his own unique dialectical hermeneutics. For the text and all its structures—generic conventions, particular plot, rhetorical figures, grammatical and linguistic foundations and procedures—produce a Self, however finally deconstructed or initially alienating, for the ego to become *like*. As Nietzsche puts it concerning the desire to "know oneself":

But how can we "find ourselves" again, and how can man "know himself"? . . . This is the most effective way: to let oneself look back on life with the question, "What have I up to now truly loved, what has drawn my soul upward, mastered it, and blessed it, too?" Set up these things that you have honored before oneself, and, maybe, they will show you, in their being and their order, a law which is the fundamental law of your own self. Compare these objects, consider how one completes and broadens and transcends and explains another, how they form a ladder on which you have all the time been climbing to your self: for your true being lies not deeply hidden in you, but [at] an infinite height above you, . . .[59]

The text, as Ricoeur makes clear, is the medium where this process of self-discovery takes place. And, as Nietzsche's language suggests, the kind of consciousness generated by the textual recovery of the self is a willful recollection of all the earlier partial identifications with one's sublime "educators," with all those figures that have heightened and universalized one's imagination. In short, Ricoeur's dialectical hermeneutics is uncannily appropriate for the study of autobiography.

The Self, then, in autobiography is clearly presented as materially and institutionally defined via the discursive structures of power in a particular culture at a particular moment in its history. Yet at the same time the unique play of linguistic and literary forms can produce, for brief moments at a time, a sense of the Self "being at the same instant predestinate and free, creation's very self" (*A*, 183). For Yeats it is essentially tragic art that can reveal this strange paradox: "All happy art seems to me . . . a hollow image of fulfilled desire, but when its lineaments express also the poverty or the exasperations that set its maker to work, we call it tragic art."[60]

Yet Ricoeur resists the Hegelian trap of positing an Absolute Subject and Absolute Knowledge as the ideal masks of the interpreter and his understanding of texts:

Far from saying that a subject already mastering his own way of being in the world projects the *a priori* of his self-understanding on the text and reads it into the text, I say that interpretation is the process by which disclosure of new modes of being—or if you prefer Wittgenstein to Heidegger, new forms of life—gives to the subject a new capacity for knowing himself. If the reference of the text is the project of a world, then it is not the reader who primarily projects himself. The reader rather is enlarged in his capacity of self-projection by receiving a new mode of being from the text itself. . . . Appropriation, in this way, ceases to appear as a kind of possession, as a way of taking hold of things; instead, it implies a moment of dispossession of the egoistic and narcissistic ego. This process of dispossessing is the work of the kind of universality and atemporality emphasized in explanatory procedures [i.e., a virtual and provisional kind]. . . . In this self-understanding, I would oppose the self, which proceeds from the understanding of the text, to the ego, which claims to precede it. It is the text, with its universal power of world disclosure, which gives a self to the ego.[61]

The vehicle for this unique act of transfiguration, an act of tragic knowledge, is not so much the symbol as metaphor.

What Ricoeur is after in this notion of the text's power of giving a self to the ego can be illuminated, I think, by what Heidegger has to say on the need for each one of us to question systematically the forms and values handed down to us by tradition, so as to retrieve the possibilities of original thinking, to repeat for ourselves in our own ways the kind of imaginative and creative work of becoming an authentic self that sees itself, in Yeats's phrase, as Oedipus must have at last: "being at the same instant predestinate and free, creation's very self."

When tradition . . . becomes master, it does so in such a way that what it 'transmits' is made to be inaccessible, proximally and for the most part, that it rather becomes concealed. Tradition takes what has come down to us and delivers it over to self-evidence: it blocks our access to those primordial 'sources' from which the categories and concepts handed down to us have been genuinely drawn. . . . Consequently, . . . Dasein no longer understands the most elementary conditions which would alone enable it to go back to the past in a positive manner and make it productively its own.[62]

For Ricoeur and for Yeats (as I will show later), the act of interpreting the texts of one's life involves this idea of creative retrieve or "repetition,"[63] in which one looks carefully at the habitual ways one has of understanding oneself as composing what Yeats calls "the tradition of myself," a tradition that must be continually put into question, so as to allow the metaphoric text of one's life to give a self to the ego.

41

This is not, however, the time to go into a full-scale treatment of Ricoeur's understanding of metaphor's role in philosophical speculation and critical interpretation, or of his differences from both Derrida and Heidegger on these matters.[64] For now, it is sufficient to say that Ricoeur believes that Derrida's "deconstruction" consists in a reduction of philosophical ideas to the aporias suggested by the "dead" metaphors buried in the philosopher's conceptual discourse, a deconstruction that is a kind of purely negative, even nihilistic Kantianism, given a linguistic twist. Ricoeur's concern is with the "living" metaphors of the poets and what the philosophic hermeneut can make of them, how he can repeat in a speculative, conceptual form the "surplus of meaning" created by "living" metaphor. For Ricoeur, metaphor is a sort of imaginative "category mistake," a poetic use of attribution (and not a simple substitution of an alien for a proper word), which first explodes the boundaries of conventional thinking with the appearance of logical contradiction and absurdity, and then builds upon these ruins a new signification that invites thought. In short, Shakespeare's famous metaphor of time as a "ravenous beggar" or Yeats's metaphor for the poet as "creation's very self" are examples of the principle of semantic innovation at work, combining two logically or conventionally antithetical meanings into a third term that is *purely* figurative, a suggestive void, however conceptually useful it may be for the dialectical thinker.

Ricoeur thus agrees with Heidegger that the poet and the thinker, though occupying different mountaintops, communicate with each other and together make culture possible.[65] Where he disagrees with Heidegger is on the question of method and the presumption that underlies Heidegger's ultimate dismissal of the idea of method, a dismissal that, for Ricoeur (unlike Gadamer), is precipitous and representative of the will-to-power that still informs the manner of Heidegger's critique of the will-to-power:

What philosopher worthy of the name prior to Heidegger has not meditated on the metaphor of the way and considered himself to be the first to embark on a path that is language itself addressing him? Who among them has not sought the 'ground' and the 'foundation,' the 'dwelling' and the 'clearing'? Who has not believed that truth was 'near' and yet difficult to perceive and even more difficult to say, that it was hidden and yet manifest, open and yet veiled? . . .[66]

Ricoeur continues in this vein for some time, turning Heidegger's own favorite weapon of interpretation, systematic interrogation, against him, to call into question every one of Heidegger's major metaphors for his manner of philosophizing. Ricoeur thus puts into question Heidegger's general rhetorical stance by disclosing in it "a will-to-power" and "a sort of vengefulness against the history of philosophy [conceived as a single finished text] which Heidegger's [own] thinking, nevertheless, calls us to renounce."[67] Ricoeur prefers a philosophical hermeneutics that would bridge the gaps that exist between the various human sciences rather than one that excavates them into chasms in the name of the Abyss of Being or, for that matter, the *mise en abîme* of deconstruction.

This desire to mediate between the different fields of the humanities motivates Ricoeur's return to Aristotle's idea of the poet as "the master of metaphor,"

who perceives power as act and act as power. He who sees as whole and complete what is sketchy and in process, who perceives . . . things as not prevented from becoming, seeing them as blossoming forth . . . every form attained as a promise of newness: In short, he who reaches "this source of the movement of natural objects, being present in them somehow, either potentially or in complete reality" (*Metaphysics* Delta 4, 1015 a 18–19), which the Greeks called phusis.[68]

This self-conscious apotheosis of the poet—itself metaphoric and symbolic by turns, like Yeats's final vision in "Among School Children"[69]—must inform the ruling idea of any comprehensive open-ended dialectic of intepretation. For such an ironic image of the poet disciplines even the most powerful suspicions of the interpreter by channeling the potential epistemological nihilism of a de Man, for instance, into a constructive appreciation of the creative possibilities of interpretation, which yet avoids the idealist bent of Abrams' version of Romanticism. Ricoeur's dialectical hermeneutics begins with a text, and submits its initial readings of that text to the history of intepretation—an action that ironically reduces the pretensions of the present in light of the recreated sublimities of the past, and so it imaginatively rediscovers the archetypal creative power of the interpreting self.[70] In *The Rule of Metaphor*, for example, Ricoeur begins with Aristotle's definition of metaphor from the *Poetics* and repeated in the *Rhetoric*, as "giving the thing a name that belong to something else; the transference being either from genus to species, or from species to genus, or from species to species, or on grounds of analogy."[71] He then traces the transformations of this Aristotelian notion from the rhetorical theory of Classical times to the grammatology of today. Ricoeur finally returns to Aristotle's views and the text of those views for continued meditation, and finds there a basis for his own idea of metaphor as creative substitution. Unlike in Hegel, Ricoeur's dialectic of interpretation never ends in the presumptuous closure of the history of interpretation in a final state of absolute self-possessing knowledge. And unlike the abysmal science of Derrida or de Man, Ricoeur's dialectical hermeneutics uncovers the productive kernel of metaphor, symbol, and myth for purposes of inspiring future speculations.

The advantage of Ricoeur's hermeneutic phenomenology for the interpereter of autobiography is substantial. Not only does his creative understanding of self-discovery enact

in the philosophical sphere the essential pattern of autobiographical reflection identified at the opening of this chapter;
but it also acts as a guide to the proper approach to characterizing rhetorically the particular knowledge generated by
the 'play' of irony in all 'self'-reflection. Following Ricoeur's
lead, one would approach autobiography in terms of the central symbol or mythic image of the creative self produced in
the course of the autobiographical inscription of a life accomplished by the differential structure of metaphors used to
define the lives of family and friends. The metaphors used
by Yeats to typify his relatives and associates form a rhetorical
structure that provokes the discovery at the site of the text
of his most necessary self-image, that central symbol of his
anti-self, much as the "figures" from "Aristotle" to "Derrida"
used by Ricoeur in *The Rule of Metaphor* to describe the different moments in the history of his subject (re-)create Aristotle's apotheosis of the poet.

The knowledge gained in this process is essentially
"tragic knowledge," like that found in *Oedipus Rex* concerning the limits of the individual will to control events, described in its unique modern form by Nietzsche as a moment
of "insight" into the irony that conditions the foundation,
development, and ends of all knowledge, including that of
science:

But science, spurred by its powerful illusion that all can be made
intelligible, speeds irresistibly toward its limits where its optimism,
concealed in the essence of logic, suffers shipwreck. For the periphery of the circle of science has an infinite number of points;
and while there is no telling how this circle could ever be surveyed
completely, noble and gifted men nevertheless reach, e'er half their
time and inevitably, such boundary points on the periphery from
which one gazes into what defies illumination. When they see to
their horror how logic coils up at these boundaries and finally bites
its own tail—suddenly the new form of insight breaks through,

45

tragic insight which, merely to be endured, needs art as a protection and remedy.[72]

This place where knowledge turns against itself and becomes tragic knowledge is the site where metaphor begins. This pattern of ironic reversal is at the center of all autobiographical reflection whatever its mode of discourse. Knowledge, to remain such, must both expose the finitude of its own roots, and affirm this situation in the imaginative projection of the tragic figure of the daimonic interpreter. As Yeats puts it: "It is in the arrangement of events as in the words, and in that touch of extravagance, or irony, of surprise, which is set there after the desire of logic has been satisfied and all that is merely necessary established, and that leaves one, not in the circling necessity, but caught up into the freedom of self-delight." What more fitting visage, after all, lies behind Ricoeur's celebration of the Aristotelian mask of the poet than that of Dionysus?

The Transfiguring Predicament

With this final question we return to our exasperating example from Yeats's *Autobiography* left hanging earlier. Thanks to Ricoeur, we can now place this example in the proper context. The generic intention of autobiography requires a continual conflict of interpretations between the designs of the autobiographer and the truth of the life. To speak strictly now: the metaphoric pattern of self-interpretation imposed upon the past life provokes the present discovery at the site of the text of that daimonic symbol of the self the writer may yet become still more and more imaginatively *like* in the future. The irony at work in autobiography is prophetic in this sense. Consider the contrast between Yeats as cocky aesthete and his cousin as criminal speculator. These metaphors compose an antithetical design of imaginative possibilities that belong to Yeats's entire autobiographical project, which leads in turn to the discovery of that symbol of the self Yeats must become *like* if he is to survive his crisis of identity and recover his creative powers. His friends and relatives become, therefore, metaphors of possible selves whose differences from one another point to and outline that "simplifying image" of the creator—Yeats's anti-self—he needs to recognize and understand.

Thus, neither Abrams' Romantic Spiral, nor de Man's Deconstructive Labyrinth, nor, for that matter, any pattern of literary history based on the idea of a Fall or of an eternal return is sufficiently comprehsive and persuasive enough to be appropriate to the open-ended dialectical narrative impulse of autobiographical reflection.[73] Rather than the closed dialectical spiral of the Romantics (at least as seen by Abrams), or the self-destructive wanderings of de Man's deconstruction, or Bloom's antithetical criticism, autobiographical reflection in a work like Yeats's follows a pattern of asymptotic approximation, as Ricoeur's own methodical self-reflection describes:

I shall not try to construct a systematic answer to this question by starting with a dogmatic principle. Rather, I shall proceed by a series of *approximations* wherein the solution reached at one level will be rectified by bringing the initial question back into question.[74]

I use Ricoeur in this study, then, as a guide to my own series of approximations: approximations of a systematic reading of autobiographical reflection as it appears in Yeats's highly ironic text.

For my purposes here, one of the most important examples of the antithetical production of the creator figure occurs in *Per Amica Silentia Lunae* (1917). This work, written at the time of the "First Draft" of *The Trembling of the Veil*, is a visionary reverie or "mythology" devoted to the ironic relationship between the man who must suffer and the daimon who creates. I see the work as providing in miniature a complete schema, not only of the later *A Vision* (1925), but also of the pattern of Yeats's autobiographical reflection. It is, for me, a kind of supplement to that earlier example from *Reveries*, showing, as it does, the complete form of his autobiographical impluse at play.

In Section 13 of *Anima Hominis*, the first part of the reverie, Yeats discloses his portrait of the creator behind his creation that he must emulate if he is to remain imaginative and so avoid, as he grows older, the dull fate of Wordsworth. This image, in analogous forms, becomes the authoritative formulation of Yeats's "anti-self." Hero, sage, saint, lover, fool, visionary mocker of all life—all these masks must bow before that vision of the image—of all those not impossible, that is most difficult for Yeats to imitate: the writer as tragic hero, the artist as a martyr to the craft of his art, who desires, as in "Ego Dominus Tuus," an ideal reader to interpret to him the otherwise indecipherable characters of his life. That is, Yeats desires to become his own perfect reader, and to tell his life to himself:

A poet, when he is growing old, will ask himself if he cannot keep his mask and his vision without new bitterness, new disappointment. Could he if he would, knowing how frail his vigour from youth up, copy Landor who lived loving and hating, ridiculous and unconquered, into extreme old age, all lost but the favour of his Muses?

> The Mother of the Muses, we are taught,
> Is Memory; she has left me; they remain,
> And shake my shoulder, urging me to sing.

Surely, he may think, now that I have found vision and mask I need not suffer any longer. He will buy perhaps some small old

48

house, where, like Ariosto, he can dig his garden, and think that in the return of birds and leaves, or moon and sun, and in the evening flight of the rooks he may discover rhythm and pattern like those in sleep and so never awake out of vision. Then he will remember Wordsworth withering into eighty years, honoured and empty-witted, and climb to some waste room and find, forgotten there by youth, some bitter crust.[75]

Neither the heroic ridiculousness of Landor, nor the Neo-Platonic bucolics of Ariosto are fitting emblems for the authentic creator. Rather, it is the tragic war with oneself that matters. One must wrest from past experience the significance lost on youth but so necessary for the nourishment of an aging if still passionately imaginative intellect. The ironic play of cocky aesthete and criminal speculator at last produces the methodical chewer of memory, the magic chef of self-creation. By means of this kind of antithetical recollection of literary or personal pasts, Yeats submits himself to the process of self-composition and so overcomes the haunting spectre of Wordsworth. Only a tragic creator, whose work discloses the "poverty" and loss behind his compensatory ideal images, can behold the vision of his poetic labors blossoming fully into the dance of life.

> Labour is blossoming or dancing where
> The body is not bruised to pleasure soul,
> Nor beauty born out of its own despair,
> Nor blear-eyed wisdom out of midnight oil.
> O chestnut-tree, great-rooted blossomer,
> Are you the leaf, the blossom or the bole?
> O body swayed to music, O brightening glance,
> How can we know the dancer from the dance?[76]

Tragic knowledge is knowing how to ask such questions in a mock-rhetorical fashion.

In *The Autobiography*, then, Yeats presents reality as seen by those who have awakened from the common dream of the world into the vision of the inexhaustible imaginative potential of pure loss: "I shall find the dark grow luminous, the void fruitful when I understand that I have nothing, that the ringers in the tower have appointed for the hymen of the soul a passing bell."[77] As Yeats's life becomes more and more used up by his art, his art grows increasingly vital and open to even the most dreadful possibilities in the play of existence. And Yeats knowingly chooses such a course for his life. Such knowledge can be truly said to be tragic or the "last knowledge," in Yeats's phrase from *Per Amica*; for it is like that possessed (according to Hegel) by Socrates when taking the cup of hemlock, or like that possessed (according to Pater), by da Vinci when administering the "finishing" touches to the doomed *Last Supper*—a knowledge that Nietzsche refers to in the epigraph to this study: both the man and the work must die, in a certain sense become "historical", if the principle, the vision, is to live, opening up (as Ricoeur argues) within the minds of men new imaginative worlds.

Of course, Harold Bloom, the major contemporary interpreter of Yeats, would want to dispute my thesis that a study of Yeats's *Autobiography* can reveal an exemplary tragic humanism. For Bloom sees Yeats in all his mature works, however grand, as a hapless victim of the myth of historical necessity and daimonic violence put forth in quintessential form in *A Vision*, which is, in Bloom's eyes, a neo-gnostic commentary on Yeats's great Romantic precursors, Shelley, Blake, and Keats, that the anxiety of influence has made bitterly antithetical, not to say inhumane.[78] Although one can learn much from Bloom, he fails to understand that from the first in his career Yeats is experimenting with the Romantic form of internalized quest, as he experiments with all inherited literary forms, in order to play out the impulse behind such forms in his work rather than live them painfully out to the bitter end. Yeats's heroism is not that of Byron's Childe Harold; he never succumbs completely to any one of his self-images, however attractive he finds that of the gnostic seer. Rather, he emulates the nobility of the writer who offers his works, with all his images inscribed at their centers, to a world where "all things rise and fall."[79] Tragic knowledge gained from the ironic situation of writing at the end of an entire cultural tradition, as a self-conscious "last Romantic," makes Yeats more a Sophocles to the potential Oedipus in us all, than a would-be Tiresias frantically in pursuit of a tyrant to provoke, and in our age finding all too many who would wish to fill the empty throne. The critic, therefore, need not volunteer his services as a surrogate Sophocles. The pains of composition, however deceptively painless to others, allow Yeats to get each part in writing before all is ruin once again. "Let all things pass away" ironically represents the transfiguring gaiety behind all song: "'What has become perfect, everything ripe—wants to die.'"[80]

2

The Prospects of Memory

I shall not try to construct a systematic
answer to this question by starting with a
dogmatic principle. Rather, I shall proceed
by a series of *approximations* wherein the
solution reached at one level will be rectified
by bringing the initial question back into question.

—Ricoeur, *History and Truth*

"Modern wit is the only representative
of the old hero. Wit is never vanquished;
and courage is an essential part of it."

—Yeats, as quoted in Lady Gregory's
Seventy Years

Es gibt im Geistigen keine Vernichtung.

—Nietzsche, *The Will to Power*

As if in a dream, a world begins to crystallize from random
fragments of memory on the first pages of Yeats's *Reveries over Childhood and Youth:* sitting on somebody's knee
looking out an Irish window at a wall covered with cracked
and falling plaster, a wall behind which once lived an un-

known relation. Or so one is told. Looking out of a London window at Fitzroy Road where boys are playing, one, perhaps a telegraph boy, in uniform: someone to blow up the town perhaps. Or so one is told. At Sligo next, watching a mastless toy boat whose painted sides are now scratched as well as worn. So the boat looks strangely farther away, especially the scratched stern, and especially the long scratch. . . . These first memories are certainly fragmentary and isolated and contemporaneous as Yeats's introductory remarks claim. But are they really "as though one remembered some first moments of the Seven Days," as we are told?

Only if the newly created world also is at the same time an already fallen one. For it is filled with signs of radical limitation—decay, fragmentation, insensitivity, terror—one might get blown up there to hear a servant tell it. Hardly Edenic. Nor is this beginning conventional. Yeats's earliest world does not simply reflect for him his trailing clouds of glory. All these memories focus instead on his becoming enmeshed in the ruinous temporal process that seems to define his existence. Predictably, his initial response is dialectical. He tries to escape his world by seeing it recede from him. As with the boat, he focuses on his world's flaws with a vengeance, almost to the point of trance. Here the shining haze, as of the Seven Days, exists at the same time (that is, as if out of time), as the corrosive and provisional materiality of the eight. In this ambivalent context the recollecting Yeats launches his analytic pursuit of the origins of his still emerging and confused self-image. Granting such radical ambivalence surrounding his quest, it is no wonder then that Yeats directs his memories primarily to a fit audience but few, familiar with all his work, and that in the Preface he broods about the nature and shape, as well as the import, of these memories. His seems to be the paradoxical obligation to recall imaginatively the figures and incidents of a world he would much rather forget but cannot until, ironically enough, he can come to himself at last.

Childhood in such a world is an interminable night of misery that most adults make light of or talk idly about, as if their childhood had been very different, or as if they have successfully forgotten most of it. One prays and prays to die in order to escape that world—or at least Yeats does—only to begin frantically praying to live when it seems that one's first prayers are about to be answered. And yet, "nobody was unkind," Yeats says. There are no easily discernible causes for childhood unhappiness here. In fact, there are some rare bright spots: a big house with a nice garden presided over by a generally mild and reassuring grandmother who lets a frightened boy hide inside the big rooms or play outside with the frisky dogs. But still, it is there that one broods on God and personal wickedness. And there on the grounds one accidently breaks a duck's wing only to find no punishment forthcoming, nor any explanation either. Wonder of wonders: instead, one has duck for dinner. Yet there, too, a lonely child is terrified by the very presence of his fierce grandfather, even if the grown man many years later cannot recall the old man ever being really harsh—or even unkind—to him. Rather, he recalls, it was simply their custom to "fear and admire" the grandfather. Nothing more than that (*A*, 2).

Or so Yeats claims many years later. A closer look at the passage paraphrased above, however, reveals that Yeats's initial interpretation of his earliest memories is tentative, uncertain, even apparently contradictory:

There was no reason for my unhappiness. Nobody was unkind, and my grandmother has still after so many years my gratitude and my reverence. The house was so big that there was always a room to hide in, and I had a red pony and a garden where I could wander, and there were two dogs to follow at my heels, one white with some black spots on his head and the other with long black hair all over him. I used to think about God and fancy that I was very wicked, and one day when I threw a stone and hit a duck in the yard by mischance and broke its wing, I was full of wonder when I was told that the duck would be cooked for dinner and that I should not be punished. Some of my misery was loneliness and some of it fear of old William Pollexfen my grandfather. He was never unkind and I cannot remember that he ever spoke harshly to me, but it was the custom to fear and admire him. (A, 2)

The movement of the passage is puzzling. It opens with a seemingly authoritative comment: "There was no reason for my unhappiness." Then it continues with a reminiscence of a favorite childhood scene, the grounds surrounding the house. These are presided over, we learn, by the idealized figure of his beneficent grandmother. Suddenly, however, an unexpected memory of a strongly negative kind, that of his morbid broodings and the duck-stoning incident, breaks into the brief meditation on his happier childhood moments, as if in justification of his morbidity. Then this violent irruption dissolves into the child's bewilderment and wonder and the man's later, distanced amusement at the confusion of adult values which the child's naïveté helps to expose. Finally, the passage ends with a conclusion, apparently drawn from all these details, which is in support of his initial statement that there was no reason for his unhappiness, even though Yeats has just stated that "some" of his misery did have a definite cause. Yet the remembered details argue against the conclusion. It is clear that adult insensitivity to his feelings, confusions, and fears is more than reason enough for his unhappiness. Authoritative comment asserting one extreme (that there was no reason for his unhappiness) gives way to details of a scene that suggests another extreme (that there were times when he was very happy living his childhood dreams). This is then followed by a series of details that could easily be considered reasons why he had to be unhappy as a child (his loneliness, his confusion, his relatives' insensitivity). Such a complex antithetical movement is typical within and among the numbered sections of *Reveries*. Either Yeats is not in control of his method here, or else he is risking the formal enactment of his gradual discovery of that method. As we shall see, Yeatsian meditation is a form of self-interpretation, in which the mind dwells upon its own antithetical arrangements of the minute particulars of experience. The repeated imposition of this pattern, of this fundamental interpretive invention, eventually provokes the discovery of the most authentic symbol of his imaginative self—or what he calls his anti-self or simplifying image. Here the process is just being initiated and so it rather naturally maintains only an uneasy focus on Yeats's earliest autobiographical symbols, such as his grandfather.[1] Yet exactly why Yeats needs this kind of antithetical self-interpretation is somewhat of a mystery.

Ironically enough, it is the mysteries of place that provide a clue. Yeats remembers only things dramatic in themselves associated with unforgettable places (*A*, 20). He is always finding places where he would like to spend his life (*A*, 38). He even imagines people, as we have seen in the case of his grandmother, posed, as if for the portrait painter, before some symbolic background (*A*, 55). What lies behind such preoccupation? Yeats instinctively believes that there are landscapes symbolical of some spiritual condition and so inspirations to a hunger "such as cats feel for valerian" (*A*, 48). The figure posed before the significant background is, like Yeats's grandmother, the presiding presence or genius of the place, a presence promising not simply sleep but a more creative semi-conscious state suggestive of great slumbering powers. As the presiding figure more and more comes to dominate its framed world in *Reveries*, Yeats begins to recognize and then re-appropriate imaginatively the hitherto habitually projected imagoes. The result is both an increase in control over himself and his world, since such imagoes are now available for conscious manipulation as images and symbols, and a growing disappointment at the sad necessity of the whole painful and never-ending enterprise. Tragic knowledge, for Yeats, comes to those who have awakened from the common dream and have made their passion a textual reality, in compensation for the experience of real loss.

Thus in *Reveries* Yeats is portrayed as discovering a dialectical method for organizing and articulating both halves of this complex perception: "Indeed I remember little of childhood but its pain. I have grown happier with every year of life as though gradually conquering something in myself, for certainly my miseries were not made by others but were a part of my own mind" (*A*, 5). The last part is an especially cheerful prospect. But both halves of such a perception are necessary moments in an ongoing symbolic drama of self. Yeats's text becomes the place where all the central figures in his life story can come to preside over their different spots of past time, as his grandmother does over one part of his childhood memories. At the interpretive site of the text, the past is not simply recollected, it is also repeated forward, as it were, through the mediating agency of the autobiographical symbol. By re-imagining his relationships with the most significant and influential models of selfhood in his life, Yeats transforms the memory traces of those personal models, seen against the background of a special place, into symbolic figures in a dialectical psychomachia enacted in the text. His grandmother and grandfather, for example, are shown to be both determining influences on the growth of his personality and contradictory figures in the script of his life-text that he has been composing unconsciously for years. Under the pressures of making a written text he finally discovers, that is, becomes conscious of, the need to synthesize, if he can, the antitheses of his imagination within increasingly more comprehensive symbolic orders. These orders constitute Yeats's most authentic self. As a result, his self (what he terms his anti-self) is an interpretive, textual phenomenon, both his own and other, both the memory fragments that are these figures and the developing whole that relates them to each other dramatically. Like an imaginative text, Yeats's self, then, is freely there, but only in its absent-minded, multi-layered way: "now that I have written it out, I may even begin to forget it all" (*A*, viii). The daimon, in such a case, is seemingly exorcised.

The early Sligo sections of *Reveries* are dominated by the figure of Yeats's grandfather, for whom the poet was named. William Pollexfen is a proud, passionate man of action, reticent to a fault about his personal life.[2] He is a man who would dive down to check out a ship's rudder when none of his own employees, cowards all, would do so. Torn skin, typically, is the paradoxical sign of his almost miraculously inviolate manhood. No wonder then that his timid grandson confuses him with God—a fierce god who would also dispense vigilante justice at the end of a horsewhip (*A*, 3). Yeats's grandfather, then, is a central figure of both grand imaginative proportions and pure dread. He is not only a powerful man, but also a powerful stimulus to Yeats's imagination, a threat to his mental coherence, as well as an instrument for bringing into focus his earliest memories.

However, this unselfconscious hero out of Romantic tales of the sea has a great flaw: there is "something helpless about him." He is easily gulled by cleverer if weaker people. A young niece baffles the old man by saying that if she were he and he she, she would give him a doll. A servant ceremoniously gives him the gate key every night, but only after leaving the gate unlocked every night. Yeats's grandfather is almost the archetype of the strong man with a weak mind.

The entire household engages in the easy ritual of trickery needed to outwit the great Lear-like patriarch.

Such a confusing figure can only haunt the boy, causing chronic self-doubts, uncritical idolizations, and vague anxiety. And because of the inconsistency and hypocrisy surrounding the figure (a helpless god!), confusion and guilt must result. Yeats knows even then that he in fact must be one of the clever to survive, even though his imagination strongly sympathizes with his grandfather. In a nightmare, the boy "foresees" a terrible sea disaster. The next day his grandfather, to his great and guilty relief, returns from a shipwreck riding a blind horse. The rest of the people on board, whom he almost singlehandedly rescued, claim they were more afraid of the terrible old man with his oar (Ulysses?) than of the stormy sea (*A*, 6). Years later, Yeats naturally must wonder "if the delight in passionate men" in his works "is more than [a] memory" (*A*, 4) of his grandfather.

By reliving and re-imagining this ambivalent relationship with his dreadful idol, Yeats is now able to define, fix, and make conscious those features he has unconsciously projected. He can "forget" them, as it were. He is now free to discern those other qualities he lacks and still must try to compensate imaginatively for if he is to escape being one-sided. For example, while writing about his eighteenth-century ancestors, he stops to look at some miniatures. He then begins to recall how and where he first heard of his great-grandfather, John Yeats. At his Aunt Mickey's house, a house covered with creepers, he says, he first saw the crimson streak of the gladiolus and waited for its blossom with excitement in "a shut-in mysterious place where one played" in the hope that something would happen. As these associations take form, so does the figure of his aunt vividly recounting the family history.[3] Yeats now can reconstruct, with the help of both memories and miniatures the essence of the man. John Yeats, it seems, so loathed the least sign of violence he would rattle his keys long before he entered the kitchen, so that if his servants were doing wrong, they would be warned of their master's approach in plenty of time to stop. In this way, they could avoid a formal reprimand, and he a tasteless scene. Though at the time Yeats cared little for his aunt's tales, he sees that "Perhaps, too, it is only now that I can value those more gentle natures so unlike his [the grandfather's] passion and violence" (*A*, 11).

Yeats has had to work through his relationship with his grandfather, a process culminating here at the site of the text, before being able to accommodate himself to other, more sensitive natures so close to his own. Yeats is here starting to experience consciously the emergence of a symbolic drama of self, in which he can come to realize his dialectical relationship to his own imagoes. A liberating procedure. Yet there is no simple triumph. Rather the cost of Yeats's new appreciation is increased alienation. Before such comparatively absolute gentleness and courtesy, he must become more conscious of his own contrasting heaviness and clumsiness, traits of men in a declining age. Only through his imaginative recreation of an earlier period and its people can he preserve at the very least the memory of what we have lost.[4] So, too, only by manipulating the components of his self-image can he make up for his own inherent lack. In this complex way, the figure of his grandfather becomes Yeats's first major autobiographical symbol, the original one, mediating his own hermeneutical extremes of creative synthesis and analytic reduction, by being an antithetical center for his psyche.

Symptomatic of the disappointment that pervades the sections or parts of sections dealing with Sligo is a passage containing Yeats's reflections on his brother's painting "Memory Harbour."[5] Coming as they do in the middle of London meditations, Yeats's remarks seem an alien irruption. "House and anchored ship and distant lighthouse all

61

set close together in some old map" dominated by a grandfather surrogate, "the blue-coated man with the mass of white shirt"—are just suddenly there.[6] Melancholy disappointment ultimately follows the initial disquiet and excitement: "I have walked on Sinbad's yellow shore and never shall another's hit my fancy" (A, 33). A recognition of his own guilt now follows the compensating hyperbole and begins to dominate his other feelings: "I am melancholy because I have not made more and better verses" (A, 33). A textual discovery: the human imagination suffers from a mysterious and tragic inability to realize its full potential; in this case, specifically from the impossibility of recovering imaginatively the all of the self's first world, perhaps because of other long suppressed memories of that world's pain. Consciousness is now that far from home, as it were. A symbolic composition whose central figure in this case suggests his guilt-inspiring grandfather dialectically discloses a hard Yeatsian truth. Enacting such truths in his works, much as that grandfather verbally acted out what he would read,[7] enables Yeats to test out his ability to endure imaginatively his own powerfully negative feelings: by making them a text for interpretation: "I often said to myself how terrible it would be to go away and die where nobody would know my story" (A, 10).

Before such perennial human dilemmas, the young Yeats is left on his own. The breakdown of the great patriarchial ethos insures that he will be without a reliable, stable set of guides. The child's chronic unhappiness is father to the man's. For the eternal human problems of belief, sex, death, and love become insoluble dilemmas almost before Yeats can begin to think about dealing with them. The resulting self-consciousness drains the imagination's energies, producing a counter-movement of regressive fantasizing, of futile escape into his own mind: "everything became less interesting than my own thoughts" (A, 14). He then becomes impossible to teach since he is alienated by an alienating world from the very contents of his own mind. At best his thoughts can be "a great excitement," which, when he tries to concentrate, necessitate a project much like "packing a balloon into a shed in high wind" (*A*, 26). A comic plight of the wayward and impetuous will no doubt—for the distanced, mature adult. But who ever achieves that improbable ideal? Certainly not Yeats: "It is so many years before one can believe enough in what one feels even to know what the feeling is" (*A*, 69).

Yeats's own father is the immediate source of his son's sense of modern fragmentation. J. B. Yeats, a figure who dominates most of the volume, especially the London sections, is a minor Irish painter and an irresponsible landowner. Influenced by both French Impressionism and Pre-Raphaelitism, he becomes obsessed by his canvasses to the point of confusion (*A*, 17) and neglects his inherited property until it begins slipping from his family's hands (*A*, 35). Nevertheless, he makes an impressive figure of a man: opinionated, robust, full of personality—and yet so belligerently spontaneous that his views, except those of Unity of Being, of course, are liable to change in an instant as if on cue (*A*, 58). Only the ideal of style, of the ordered passion of organic forms, saves him from a direct perception of his own apparently hopeless fragmentation.

His is the monstrous image of the Victorian papa, an angry and impatient judge and teacher whose very presence is meant to intimidate. His black beard and hair, his cheek bulging from a fig for a bad tooth, soon perhaps from a live frog (or so Yeats's nursemaids suggest—*A*, 14)—all these details are fraught with the threat of violence. To conquer his son's own spontaneous and wandering mind, his paternal duty will even let him fling a book at that tender head (*A*, 14). Pure hypocrisy of course. Rather than let the boy enjoy the easy pleasures of Euclid (!), he must terrorize him into learning absurd Latin lessons by vividly comparing his potential degeneration with that of actual and literary low-lifes (*A*, 37). And yet, from his father's constant badgering, Yeats does seem to develop a conscience. The voice of his conscience comes to him at moments of crisis to repudiate specific words or deeds, whether actual or imagined. Like Socrates' daimon, it never tells him directly what to do or to believe. Yeats must discern that dialectically from the shape of the accumulated repudiations (*A*, 5–6). This is an important interpretive acquisition, informing what has been termed Yeats's "affirmative capability."[8] Imaginatively testing out possible self-images at the point of crisis to find the truly necessary one: such, in essence, is the Yeatsian response to fragmentation. So his father, it seems, has provided his son with some basis for interpreting his world after all.

Reviewing now his alienation in London, Yeats begins to see the emerging necessary pattern. Though at the mercy of skilled toughs when thrown as a stranger with different mental images into a second-rate British boy's school, Yeats, after first longing to escape into his memories of Sligo ("I longed for a sod of earth . . . something of Sligo to hold in my hand"—*A*, 19), then reacts more affirmatively. He uses his reputation, built on pretense, for easily holding his breath underwater and for running the longest races without great strain to win over the school's leading athlete, who proceeds now to fight the weaker, more excitable boy's battles for him (*A*, 24). Projecting the right self-image pays off for Yeats it seems. Similarly, when his father directly spoils his dream of becoming a great athletic hero by meanly recounting how a too sensitive ship's purser's hair turned white at the battle of Trafalgar, the self-conscious boy is forced to turn his attention to the original sources of his dream's inspiration: the precise wording of the phrase he read lauding "the bright particular star of American athletics" (A, 24) and his pen and ink sketches of himself covering the white squares of his chessboard, which portray him "doing all kinds of courageous things" (A, 25). Attending to and being able to manipulate the elements, linguistic or pictorial, that constitute one's self-images clearly seems to be necessary now.[9] His father then has "helped" the boy again—at least to come to an early if painful recognition of the compensatory and defensive function of the imagination, especially in a bad time. Re-experiencing these humiliating self-discoveries, Yeats irrupts into an adamant but useless protest against the cruel discrepancy between one's imaginative potential and the actual state one has achieved. This later protest, amplifying an early insight, underscores the clear continuity between boy and man on this central point: "I was vexed and bewildered, and am still bewildered and vexed, finding it a poor and crazy thing that we who have imagined so many noble persons cannot bring our flesh to heel" (A, 25). Yeats's interpretive method reveals the antitheses of his mental development with the result that the continuity of his personality is revealed, even if the continuity is one of deepening disappointment.

On the ultimate questions of religious belief, sexuality, love, death, and the purpose of the human imagination, Yeats's father, through his opposition or neglect, makes his son become, finally, more self-reliant—but at a great cost. Though he desperately needs to believe, to have those cloudy glimpses of luminous sky portend a possible divine communication (A, 15), his father is a doctrinaire non-believer, of course. This conflict inspires perpetual brooding on serious matters, even as a young child (A, 15). Because of his father's lack of guidance, for example, he is forced to conclude that it must be God's direct intervention behind the mysteries of creation: "God would bring the calf in the cloud out of the light" (A, 16). He then is easily shattered when he learns of the "mechanism of sex." It is "the first breaking of the dream of childhood" (A, 16). Typically enough, he doubts the direct testimony on the matter from what he terms an older boy's "pathic" (A, 16), only to become convinced by the authoritative text of an encyclopedia entry (A, 16). Similarly, when his younger brother Robert dies, Yeats learns of death's terror not directly from his father's example, but indirectly yet more powerfully for him from the story his mother and a servant tell of the banshee crying the night the little boy died (A, 16). (Yeats's initial, inadequate response is to make toy boats with their flags at half-mast.) So his father's neglect, in this case, leads to his son's discovery that dread of death cannot be escaped, nor should it be, since our response to it testifies to the authenticity of our dread and our love.

Finally, even when it comes to poetry, Yeats's father lets the contradictions inherent in his own conflicting reactions hit his young son head on, without any thought of the needed synthesis.[10] On the one hand, Yeats's impressionable young mind instinctively absorbs from his father's celebration of poetry as drama the awareness that it can give him models, like Hamlet, Manfred, or even Alastor, whose self-possession, or at least self-dedication, might provide, if emulated, a defense against the inner fragmentation, and so give his imagination centers of attention suggestive of an ideal satisfaction. Through the medium of textual creation, one just might attain a perfect identity of the kind that exists between childhood friends engaged in imaginatively acting out a shared adventure: "their minds become one and the last secret disappears" (A, 31). Perfect self-transparency within the highly differentiated interior becomes the almost impossible goal of Yeats's poetic quest. On the other hand, his father explicitly singles out (to be scorned) poetry that thins the blood and dries up the humanity in young boys because of its abstract ideals. Rather than permit his son to write a paper on Tennyson's "'Men may rise on stepping stones of their dead selves to higher things,'" (*sic*), a line on the face of it in accord with some of his father's tastes, he insists that the boy defy his teacher (this one time of course!) and write instead, ironically enough, on Polonius's "'To thine own self be true'" (*A*, 37). The boy naturally remains baffled.

The ultimate effect of such confusing schooling on the boy is to inspire in him the accumulation and securing of defensive mechanisms, though he senses even at this age that his father's inconsistencies and his own defensiveness have already tended to victimize him in many ways. At this point in the text Yeats expands that implicit recognition into a major polemic full of the illusory ideals and painful realities of nostalgia and bitter regret:

He should have taken me away from school. He would have taught me nothing but Greek and Latin, and I would now be a properly educated man, and would not have to look in useless longings at books that have been, through the poor mechanism of translation, the builders of my soul, nor face authority with the timidity born of excuse and evasion. Evasion and excuse were in the event as wise as the house-building instinct of the beaver (*A*, 38).

Characteristically, Yeats makes a revolution in point of view turn on a change in the style of his text. Though still starved for the great originals of his imaginative life, he can nevertheless approach that instinctive fitness he assumes they possess and the unmediated vision they dispense through the construction and elaboration of such symbolic complexes as found here. In the sign of the beaver he shall conquer! The above passage in fact suggests that perhaps J. B. Yeats's erratic ways might not be the worst approach to raising a child, for the boy has had to figure out for himself from the different and difficult "texts" of each crisis which interpretation is correct for him. Like his mother who delights in the momentary conjunctions of cloud textures (*A*, 40), or his grandmother who becomes passionately absorbed in the intricate toils of her flower-tracings (*A*, 4), Yeats realizes, and unlike them can articulate, the idea that he must labor over the texts of himself if he is to discover there the identity, amid the differences, in his life-long drama of symbolic interpretation. As Yeats discovers from his misreading the text from Solomon that inspired his fruitless scientific pursuits (*A*, 41), and as his father's painter friends (Wilson, Page, Nettleship, and Potter), should have learned from the failure of their creative lives ("the Romantic movement drawing to its latest phase"—*A*, 29), one must become a single-minded maker of texts, taking as imaginative models first other maker's creations, then one's own, and finally the image of the creator itself. Ironically yet fittingly, Yeats's unique imaginative development really begins here with his recognition that he has misread a text: "I came to believe that I had gone through so much [fruitless] labour because of a text . . ." (*A*, 41).

Under his father's weird regime, then, Yeats has learned (and now relearned for himself) that the intricacies of personal relations have a dialectical and symbolic cast and that the imagination must function to compensate for his time's fragmentation, as well as it must try to meet the chronic human problems, through the creation and manipulation of the changing texts of one's possible self-images. Imaginatively repeating the past, especially his early London experiences, helps him to realize the significance of his life-long antithetical conflict of autobiographical symbols, whose outcome is a confrontation with the only necessary one: that of the creator: A long quotation provides a good if unadorned example of Yeats's dialectical method fully under control.[11] In accord with reveries, this whole section suddenly appears in the text without any obvious preparation:

Two pictures come into my memory. I have climbed to the top of a tree by the edge of the playing field, and am looking at my school-fellows and am as proud of myself as a March cock when it crows to its first sunrise. I am saying to myself, "If when I grow up I am as clever among grown men as I am among these boys, I shall be a famous man." I remind myself how they think all the same things and cover the school walls at election times with the opinions their fathers find in the newspapers. I remind myself that I am an artist's son and must take some work as the whole end of life and not think as the others do of becoming well off and living pleasantly. The other picture is of a hotel sitting-room in the Strand, where a man is hunched up over the fire. He is a cousin who has spec-ulated with another cousin's money and has fled from Ireland in danger of arrest. My father has brought us to spend the evening with him, to distract him from the remorse that he must be suf-fering. (*A*, 26–27)

The first image is what we would expect from the defensive, alienated son of a foreign artist. To seek to be "well off," and not all in all in the toil of one's life-long aesthetic work, would be to become inauthentic, abstract, and rhetorical, even for the young boy. His cleverness has freed him from the fate of his school-fellows: not to possess their own minds. The second image clearly is a negative exemplum of just such inauthenticity. And yet, it is more than that, for it also sug-gests that the cleverness Yeats celebrates for the apparent triumph it has brought and still might bring him can also lead, when it becomes aggressive and externalized, to crim-inality and defeat. Even more importantly, in the figure of the cousin hunched up over the fire, who one must assume feels remorse (for one never knows about such clever men who manipulate appearances), Yeats also sees a warning of what his own cleverness could do to his ability to know and express his own feelings. If he does not face his present identity crisis without the hollow solace of clever defenses, then his fate seems clear. By juxtaposing these two pictures, one representing his inflated "cocky" self-dedication to art, the other suggesting the depressing dangers of that dedication for him, Yeats uses his cleverness against itself to check his tendency to egotistic inflation. He symbolically amplifies certain latent significances of these memory traces (for surely no young boy said such things to himself in this fashion), in order to project a supplementary drama of self-interpretation. Lacking one informing interpretive principle ("I had as many ideas as I have now, only I did not know how to choose from among them those that belonged to my life"—*A*, 55), Yeats must constantly alter the established perspective of consciousness by summoning up, through the process of textual creation, that of the unconscious. This unexpected, irrational, buried perspective ultimately forms the basis for the discovered design of the autobiographical project: "Looking backwards, it seems to me that I saw my father's mind in fragments, which has always hidden connections I only now begin to discover" (*A*, 43). As always, Yeats is speaking antithetically, that is, primarily of himself here. The compensating relationship that exists between the conscious points of view and the unconscious insights is fully realized only at the site of the text. Paradoxically enough, the perception of the necessity in his own imaginative development evolves from Yeats's most unpredictable symbolic utterances. Design, in short, seems to evolve from chance, to actualize Yeats's desire to be.

The last, largely Dublin sections of *Reveries* focus on Yeats's gradual approach to his first successful imaginative model, John O'Leary. O'Leary is, like Yeats's grandfather, the strong and passionate man of action. But he is also, unlike the old man and like Yeats's father, articulate. Unlike both, however, he is generous and morally sensitive as well. Yet Yeats cannot simply emulate him, as if he were only the schematization of the required synthesis. Rather he has to appropriate his image imaginatively. That is, he must completely absorb it into the original core of his self-interpretation, finally assimilate it once and for all. But before he can, he somehow must work free of his father's still overpowering influence (A, 42). By moving from one potential model to another Yeats is more and more able to stand on his own. This is true for the young man and the older poet. In these sections, we see the youth develop into a man even as we see the man relive the dubious as well as the real achievements of that painful development. The later Yeats, re-imagining the earlier "progress," is able to clarify and systematize the tentative insights into the necessity of his own imaginative nature.

Yeats's uncle George Pollexfen, astrologer, ceremonial magician, and hypochondriac, is the first apparently unlikely model. This patient man comes to replace Yeats's impetuous and irascible grandfather in the company when the old man retires, and in Yeats's imagination during the youth's Sligo summers. He likes everything neat and compendious "as upon shipboard" (A, 44), and he is the classic "happy" complainer: the Celtic ironist whose joy is to live in perpetual despondency, "sighing every twenty-second of June over the shortening of the days" (A, 45). Such ability to relate opposites, to bring the cycle of time into ironic focus can become a silly gift indeed, and yet Yeats needs to acquire this ability, too. He did so instinctively then under his uncle's influence, and must do so consciously now as a man alone. For the slight distance from the world such irony creates allows the overly sensitive to take command in a crisis, as his uncle does, when he must steer a ship through a difficult gap in the channel wall after his many years on land (A, 44). The ability to take command is just what Yeats still needs now during the imaginative crisis in his life. Slow, diligent method (A, 45) also underlies this ability, with the result that "this inactive man, in whom the sap of life seemed to be dried away," mysteriously possesses "a mind full of pictures" (*A*, 45). Yeats's great devotion to the strict requirements of a craft and his compulsive need to remake himself and his style might have their origin here in the example of this methodological ironist.[12]

Similarly, in Edward Dowden the young Yeats instinctively sees something he needs: an image of "the sage," who uses his dark romantic beauty and good-humored irony to hide an unexpectedly bitter life as well as to fend off easily and so effectively neutralize by his example the youth's unanswerable and self-torturing philosophical questions: a Dublin, handsome Socrates.[13] And yet Dowden is ultimately unsatisfactory, for his poetic emotions are conventional, his critical judgments suspect, and his famous irony an intellectualized defense for timidity.[14] That irony does not lead, like the gay exaggeration of the Pre-Raphaelities, to the discovery of truth. Instead, it hides inner division.

For example, his harmless effusions over Shelley's poetry are the result of a senseless devotion to duty, "the violence and clumsiness of a conscientious man hiding from himself a lack of sympathy" (*A*, 58). In him, one extreme fathers another with no meaningful relationship established between them. His sly smile of intellectual condescension is really a sign of his giving up the fight. He is finally "provincial" and not of the "free world" (*A*, 59). Yeats's father sees in him an image of the fate he escaped (*A*, 56).[15] He is finally right on Dowden: the latter is like a priest who should not be reminded of his sacrifice. Yet, as a young man, Yeats assimilates unconsciously an important lesson from him, one his father could not teach him, and one he only now can understand. To write successful lyric poetry a man must let himself be shaped by both nature and art, so he can adopt not one pose but many ("lover or saint, sage or sensualist, or mere mocker of all life"—*A*, 59), and then relate them to one another as in a play of opposites. The result hoped for is "that stroke of luckless luck" which "can open before [us all] the accumulated expression of the world" (A, 57). For the center of the drama is the imagination itself, that silent zone, in which language begins to speak as if with tongues of fire.

The dialectical interaction of selves between the poet's complex textual creation and the reader's critical interpretation creates that "absence in reality" Wallace Stevens speaks of through which all a people's possible worlds can begin to emerge.[16] In this passage (A, 57), memory traces are symbolically amplified. This is the essence of Yeats's interpretive method in *The Autobiography*. Each element in the composition of the text can act as an irritant to stimulate the ultimately conscious appropriation of an instinctive symbolic structure. Yeats's self is reunited with its own "emanations" at last. Dowden himself becomes a double-meaning symbol, initially a guide for the youth and now a warning to the man. He becomes a text whose possible interpretations remain latent until Yeats's antithetical imagination activates the set of opposing meanings necessary at a particular time in his life. Dowden thus is turned into a generative sign that a complex readjustment and balancing of Yeats's own view of himself is in process. The other person, in effect, is only "other" in terms of the possible differences in Yeats's continuing self-interpretation. When Yeats interprets other people, he transforms them into figures that receive their life from the excess of his own personal significance that he projects into them, an excess that in any one interpretation cannot be completely fathomed or systematized, and so figures such as Dowden seem both similar to and different from Yeats. It is from him that they receive their life.

Mohini Chatterjee, the Indian swami, is not so much a solid center for Yeats's next stage of personal development as a sign of his growing independence. His doctrine, at once "logical and boundless" (A, 61), that consciousness is not just pure surface but also has heights and depths, provides philosophical justification for Yeats's psychic research and mystical speculations, activities which finally are to free him from his father's influence (*A*, 59). Yeats, as founder of the Hermetic Society, now can face rather than hide from disapproving authority figures.[17] He also proposes a doctrine for the membership to explore. It is his first systematization of formerly provisional insights. Believe "whatever the great poets affirmed in their finest moments" (*A*, 60), and that is the closest one can come now to authoritative religion and to truth. For truth is "'the dramatically appropriate utterance of the highest man'" (*A*, 60). Different points of view are not necessarily mutually exclusive, but rather, can be symbolically true to the imaginative situation out of which they arise, truth changing as the situation changes, as another stage is reached. And "'the highest man'"? Yeats now glosses this idea as a limit concept: "'We can but find him as Homer found Odysseus when he was looking for a theme'" (*A*, 60). Out of a people's accumulated expression (embedded by language in the poet's unconscious, itself primarily a stratified linguistic formation), a figure of that man starts taking shape, forming itself out of the material found there, like some fabulous embryo, that of the tragic creator. For our age this figure is that of the creator heroically overcoming his own inner fragmentation to create imaginative works that suggest the same possibility is open to all of us. But according to which one of the many genetic models? This is the nagging question of unity that defines Yeats's chronic imaginative dilemma.

Uncertainty about the nature of the self causes Yeats continual self-doubt—naturally enough. This self-doubt expresses itself, despite his growing independence, in a feeling that he lacks self-possession: "I wished to become self-possessed, to be able to play with hostile minds as Hamlet played, to look in the lion's face, as it were, with unquivering

74

eyelash" (*A*, 62). Because Yeats has not realized yet that the much-vaunted self-possession is solely an internal condition,[18] he tries to gain it by joing Mr. Oldham's debating club: in order to be "schooled" out of his self-consciousness. There he meets John O'Leary, with whom he soon comes to live. O'Leary and his sister, Ellen, are fit to be counted among "Plutarch's people." No fanaticism or bitterness mar her gentleness or his generosity,[19] though both have every right to a reasonable share of each, especially, of course, the once jailed and exiled Fenian leader.

It is O'Leary who saves Yeats from his unconsciously adopted and exaggerated Dowden pose, which he has consciously rejected. Saying violent and paradoxical things just to shock provincial sobriety is merely a provincial version of a sophisticate's *epater le bourgeois*. O'Leary's "moral genius," his insistence that there are some things one cannot do no matter what the rationale or fashion, captivates Yeats. He sees in that genius something as "spontaneous as the life of the artist": it becomes Yeats's delight "to rouse him to these outbursts for I was the poet in the presence of his theme" (*A*, 64). O'Leary allows Yeats for the first time to imagine assuming the role of creator behind such a figure and his grand utterances. It is not that the aging poet again wants to be like O'Leary in the political world, but that he must reabsorb the lesson of that energy and command—how it is balanced by gentleness and courtesy, how it is conserved by being expended only on the deepest convictions: in Yeats's case, these enabling devices and habits of mind that help his imagination survive its own fragmentation. O'Leary is Yeats's original "highest man" at the point when he needs to become conscious of his own creative potential in the world of imagination. Yeats has found a central theme at last.

O'Leary's foil is John F. Taylor, an "obscure, great orator," who is gentle and deferential with the old Fenian, but "a savage animal" in argument with others: rhythm-drunk with his own elaborate rhetoric (*A*, 65). Much like both his gullible grandfather and great-voiced father,[20] Taylor fascinates and haunts Yeats, who sees the orator primarily as "the tragic figure" of his youth, so "imprisoned in himself," in his own rhetorical creations, that, like a Dutch doll, he keeps getting wound up only to be left to run down again. Clearly Taylor exists for Yeats, both then and now, as an emblem of a possible fate if he does not treat his own rhetorical disease with strong doses of self-irony. For example, because of all O'Leary's support,[21] Yeats begins to feel more self-confident, finding the time to be ripe for him to plot and scheme to set his seal on the wax-like Irish situation. He dreams of creating "a universal, symbolic art" out of the particulars of his country's fragmentation, an art that would bring together the vulgar and passionate as well as the noble and disinterested halves of the population through the synthesis of traditional Irish literary beauties and a contemporary European pose—all with the help of an exacting self-criticism. The art would be a "new and healing Eleusis" (*A*, 68). Yeats's inability at the time to combine his father's dramatic with his own lyric aesthetic should have argued against such a grand conception (*A*, 68), but his rhetorical daimon had completely caught him up. As he realizes now most of the poems written out of this politically compromised situation are flawed: "when I re-read those early poems which gave me so much trouble, I find little but romantic convention, unconscious drama" (*A*, 69). Yeats's youthful project of uniting Ireland is an instance of projecting into the political sphere an effort at attaining the necessary order that has to be made first within oneself.

The final image we have of Yeats at this time argues as much. Attending a seance at the house of a young man about to be arrested under suspicion of Fenianism, Yeats at first resists the "supernatural" experience, fearful of losing control over his own will. But then he becomes the vehicle for a great and violent energy that breaks up the table and generally disturbs the whole house. Terrified, he tries to pray, but no longer knowing any prayers, he recites instead the opening lines of Milton's *Paradise Lost*, upon the hearing of which the spirits, perhaps disciples of Poe, desert the house immediately. In his boyish vanity, Yeats at first believe it is he who banished them (*A*, 70). Yeats's subsequent and more considered response to the whole incident is indicative of the timidity, uncertainty, and duality of mind that, fortunately for us at least, are ever to haunt the creator in him:[22] "For years afterwards I would not go to a seance or turn a table and would often ask myself what was the violent impulse that had run through my nerves? was it part of myself—some thing always to be a danger perhaps; or had it come from without, as it seemed?" (*A*, 70). That the necessary, and sad, answer to both parts of the question can be yes is the wisdom the later Yeats must still learn. Experiencing part of himself only as an alien, impulsive, overpoweringly violent influx is the danger.[23]

Reveries, however, does not end on this note. Rather, both the death of Yeats's grandparents and the publication of his first book of poems (O'Leary providing the subscribers) mark the end of his childhood and the real beginnings of his independence. There are signs, however, that such independence is not only hard won but very fragile. When he visits his dying grandfather, illness "refining" that hero's face, the old childish fear to run away from him overtakes Yeats, and he leaves almost immediately thereafter. But there are also other signs that what independence Yeats now has might be easily lost because of external forces over which he could never have any control. As soon as the old man dies, the servants, who always seemed above suspicion, begin pilfering the house, getting away with worthless stuff for the most part. An absurd phenomenon.[24] Both the tentative inner balance and the decaying traditional order, then, seem about to face even greater threats of collapse. And for the first time, Yeats sees in his uncle's habitual tolerance and generalized concern for others a low view of human nature that never brings out the best in people because it always secretly expects the worst. Against such a baleful background, only the publication of Yeats's first set of poetic texts appears to stand out as a center around which he may gravitate; a volatile center, however, weakened by many immature and compromised poems.

Given this context, Yeats's conclusion to this first volume of his autobiography is not really that odd, even though it has sparked many and various, perhaps eccentric interpretations.[25] It deserves the attention it has gotten, however, primarily because it suggests that in 1914–1915 Yeats feels a deep dissatisfaction with his life, and, by implication, with his artistic rendering of that life. Though he has lived now with his own youth and childhood daily for many months, has sought to mimic the growth of his own mind by his meditative symbolic style, and has begun to disclose and make conscious his instinctive dialectical method of imaginatively surviving the fragmentation of his age, he still feels disturbed and sorrowful. Quite simply, he is disappointed because the actual realization of his imaginative potential does not live up to the prospect of realizing it. To put it another way, there is a large discrepancy, a great gulf between the rich possibilities and the poor reality. All the work and worry (his own and the family's) to defend, develop, and clarify his imagination does not seem to balance for him the achievement so far. And this result does not seem to be taken by him as atypical, or only typical of the stage of life he is reflecting on, but rather as representative of the human condition: "All life weighed in the scales of my own life seems a preparation for something that never happens" (A, 71). The ghost of Shelley's fading coal haunts Yeats here.

It would be simplistic and inflexible to conclude that *Reveries* organizes itself around three places, Sligo, London, and Dublin, as if around three clearly defined stages in Yeats's early development, according to some neat academic version of Blake's progression of innocence, experience, and the beginning of wisdom. For surely Yeats's childhood begins already fractured by the divisions of experience. Nevertheless, there is a general tendency, qualified by Yeats's shuffling back and forth in his memory between these different places, toward such a distinction of stages in his early life. The thing that must be remembered is that Yeats seems to begin life with the sense of a fall already imprinted on his mind. The result is that any simplistic reading of a Blakean scheme into the work would have to be adjusted radically for the bleaker, even more threatening context. Yeats's childhood does have its spots of innocence amid all the pain, those shut-in mysterious places, for example, those places upon which the interpretive site of the text is modeled. But there is no pervasive, joyous glow. Similarly, since Blake's time, the pressures of experience have grown even as the possibilities for wisdom have shrunk. So, in *Reveries*, one must say that Yeats begins with his victimization by his time, then moves slowly toward his achievement of some control over himself and his world, enough to face the chronic human problems of existence with some self-possession, and finally focuses on his becoming creative: on his poet's quest. All the while, however, his growing imagination has been deepening his tragic awareness of human existence, an awareness symbolically amplified by his later interpretation. Yeats's seems to be almost a modern, ironic adaptation of the ancient Gnostic vision. Only at the site of the text do the original traces of possible self-images remain, like sacred relics or precious fossils, to be lovingly uncovered, retrieved, and reconstructed, so as to be all too painfully understood, when analyzed for what prospects they hold for discovering the truly significant features of that one still other and solely necessary self: "I did not care for mere reality and believed creation should be deliberate, and yet I could only imitate my father" (*A*, 55).[26]

Tragic knowledge emerges from Yeats's dialectical interpretation of his life and times, from his initial feelings of fragmentation and alienation to his more recent sense of universal collapse. Yeats's hope is to find, in Ricoeur's phrase, "a central symbol of self" that can survive the cycles of change and that underlies the antithetical vision of himself and his world.

3

The Genius of Technique

All art is in the last analysis an endeavour
to condense as out of the flying vapour
of the world an image of human perfection,
and for its own and not for the art's sake,
and that is why the labour of the alchemists,
who were called artists in their day, is a befitting
comparison for deliberate change of style.
—Yeats, Preface to the *Collected Poems*,
In the Seven Woods, 18 May 1906

We achieve, if we do achieve, in little
sedentary stitches. . . .
—Yeats, *The Autobiography*, p. 104

A charming world of self-conscious Romance: crooked, winding streets, a child's playground of unfinished, "old-fashioned" houses, cooperative stores with seventeenth-century window-panes—all brooded over protectively by great shadow-casting chestnut trees: "the pre-Raphaelite movement at last affecting life" (*A*, 76). So London's Bedford Park appears in Yeats's boyhood. But when the young man returns there with the family at the end of the eighties, he discovers that "exaggerated criticism" has taken "the place of enthusiasm" as if in the natural course of things. Innumerable reports and rumors of leaky roofs, chronically stopped drains, cheap houses, and so on. Even the cooperative stores lose their romance under the circumstances. And the Tabard Inn, styled after Chaucer's, is now "so plainly a common public house," for "its great sign of a trumpeter designed by Rooke, the pre-Raphaelite artist, had been freshened by some inferior hand" (A, 75). The recollecting poet, years later, can only indicate his defensive suspicion that such is the fate of an ideal in the changing world, especially in a highly critical and "realistic" one like ours, by ironically describing those streets as "ostentatiously picturesque" and by cynically recalling the opinion of an architect friend of his father's, that the wooden balustrade on the local church's slanting roof "had been put there to keep the birds from falling off" (A, 75).

In response to this world where the passive but technically perfect realism of Carolus Duran and Bastien Lepage is offered as a model for would-be artists, the young Yeats, unlike his more indecisive father, sticks to his boyhood favorites: Blake and Rossetti and their celebration of the creative imagination's absolute saving power over the universe of death. Though he can understand the criticism of the younger generation, that its fathers wasted their genius on too many things, on imitating too many and undisciplined visionary models, Yeats cannot feel part of his time, for it only looks before it "with the mechanical gaze of a well-drilled soldier" (A,76) toward a dismal proletarian future, its empty revolutionary and welfare rhetoric promising a literally impossible, universal salvation.

On top of disappointment and conflict, the youthful Yeats is further alienated from his own age by being deprived, thanks to Huxley and Tyndall, of the simple-minded religion of his childhood—perhaps a necessary but nonetheless cruel deprivation since it is premature. For unlike most others of his generation, he says, he now responds to his situation by creating "an infallible Church of poetic tradition," a collection of stories, personages, and emotions passed on in nearly their original forms by poets and painters from their anonymous beginnings among the people: "with some help from philosophers and theologians" (A, 77). This world, which he hoped one day could indeed be discovered perpetually even in the "tiles around the chimney piece" (A, 77), has for its center a belief in the normative function of visionary creations, like Shelley's Prometheus. Whatever one can imagine them saying must be the nearest one can come now to truth. Yeats's Church has only this "one" doctrine. These "imaginary people" are created out of "the deepest instinct of man, to be his measure and his norm." In short, since the world is a war of fragments, Yeats seeks order at first, and recurrently, in the Romantic idea of a life steeped in one grand visionary whole. Some apocalyptic "perfect final event" (A, 77) must transform the world radically according to the imperial designs of our chronically frustrated desires, a transformation heralded, for Yeats, by the most imaginative of those "imaginative people." Yet, again, the recollecting poet comments ironically on this war of interpretations between his young self and the rest of the modern world: "at seventeen years old I was already an old-fashioned brass cannon full of shot, and nothing had kept me from going off but a doubt as to my capacity to shoot straight" (A, 77). As we shall see, Yeats must come to build his life on such playful, saving nothings.

In this early context, when a beautiful young woman, whose complexion is luminous "like apple blossoms through which the light falls" (A, 82), arrives at the family house and praises war, "not as the creator of certain virtues but as if there were some virtue in excitement itself" (A, 82); how can the shy young Yeats resist taking her side eagerly, especially when it vexes his father to do so? For here is a vision promising an end to the painful complexities of consciousness: abandon yourself to the thrill of the battle with little thought of the ultimate purpose or the cost; use all causes, no matter how great, for the excitement they generate. "What matter?" Yeats's vision of Maud Gonne seems to suggest. But the later Yeats can now see the cost if not all of the purpose. Then he could see only her beauty, not hear all her words, really hear them, and so, ironically, his own aesthetic fascination saves him finally from her fate. What once was a singular beauty worthy of the Virgilian commendation, "She walks like a goddess," now is prematurely the haunting hollow-eyed form of some Euripidean Sybil. Then a classical impersonation of Spring; now this. In between are all the rapid and prematurely wearying and debilitating passages "to and fro" between Dublin and Paris, for some political affairs. Always poignantly surrounded by many and strange pets, "by cages full of birds, canaries, finches of all kinds, dogs, a parrot, and once a full-grown hawk from Donegal" (A, 82), she is helter-skelter in her life style, much to her own despair, as well as to that of friends, even to strangers. Though initially and recurrently for years afterward Maud's image drains Yeats of his imaginary energy, that image also serves finally as a warning to avoid her fate and an inspiration for his work. Maud Gonne becomes for him a prime example of our modern "tragedy." Under all that beauty and energy lies hidden a mind that, Yeats comes to see years later, had to take "a mess of shadows" for its meat. Only a boiling stew of ruinous abstractions, strangely enough, can seem to stimulate her. Though in his poems time could only make her magically more beautiful when Yeats imagines it touching her form, in our fragmented age, which exacerbates time's evil effects on individual genius, it must make her hopelessly, if still nobly, old.[1]

Maud Gonne, typical of Yeats's other friends from his past, becomes for the recollecting poet of *The Trembling of the*

Veil the means whereby he now can compose and project into the future his antithetical self-identity. She, and all the rest of them, are the recollected perceptual occasions for the development of a symbolic dialectic. By making his friends over into completed images of his own latent and potentially disastrous tendencies, Yeats can at last bring to culmination the previously unconscious project of self-definition, clearly in opposition to their own crisis-ridden, truncated development—once all is made conscious in the text. He comes to discover fully from what they seem to lack what he must be and still must strive to become even more completely if he is to continue to survive imaginatively. His friends become primarily then negative *exempla*. This is true even when Yeats suggests that if certain of their qualities, which he also shares and successfully exploits, had not been left unexploited or incompletely exploited, their genius, too, might have survived or even prospered. The role of negation in the determination of his own identity, then, always remains central. If Lionel Johnson, that skilled and austere poetic technician, had not also been driven to drink by his absurdly inhuman ascetic ideal . . . Mediating opposites demands more flexibility from the imagination than this, if it is to survive its own divisions. Or so Yeats learns and will continue to learn from his other autobiographical symbols. In a world seemingly defined by strife and discord, by the war of one fragmentary point of view against another, of each against all and all against each, the story of one's life must become in the process an implicit psychomachia at least. The hope is that the necessary projected oppositions, created in response to other combatants, as well as to one's own psychic disorder, may progressively lead to greater self-knowledge and to stronger imaginations.[2] Bouncing off one another, if only in the playground of each other's mind, is a process that can sharpen, thicken, and make wiry the individual psyche's ideal bounding outline. This is the way, in any case, of

Yeats's aggressive interpretive invention. Yeats's self-differentiation and identity, so much in peril in a rapidly changing world, might be assured thereby—however costly that assurance tallies up to be in Yeats's own unillusioned eyes. Hence that knowing, defensive irony that pervades the beginning of Yeats's most extensive and systematic self-interpretation so far.

Near the conclusion of "Four Years: 1887–1891," the first book of *The Trembling of the Veil*, Yeats breaks off the narrative of his life to identify specifically his major autobiographical symbols. Of all the characters introduced in this first act of his five-act tragic drama, this play of interpretation,[3] it is Henley, Wilde, and Morris to whom he looks primarily for self-definition. He points out the implicit differences between their and his own anti-self. The anti-self, Yeats tells us here, is that "image"—"always opposite to the natural self or the natural world"—which the individual projects into his life and work, either consciously or unconsciously, depending on the degree of self-knowledge. Once discovered, it must be "copied," that is, rigorously lived up to in every thought and deed (*A*, 115)—to my mind as if in imitation of a divine model. The anti-self is also called "our simplifying image, our genius," in the original sense of that term, and as might be expected, "such hard burden does it lay upon us that," like an almost impossible ego-ideal, "but for the praise of others, we would deride it and hunt it away" (*A*, 81).

Henley, the first of Yeats's major symbols, is for him the inarticulate cripple who dreamt himself a vigorous and heroically self-possessed aristocrat, vainly seeking in the modern world the establishment of a tyranny much like Cosimo de Medici's (*A*, 84). Wilde, on the other hand, is the man of action who dreamt himself a fanciful aesthete in order to master, through the sharp barb of his facile wit and sure swordsman-like poise, the polite monsters of Imperial London's most important dinner tables (*A*, 91). Finally, Morris, no synthesis, is the rough and loveless but strangely beloved great beast of a man (in this regard much like Yeats's grandfather), who dreamt himself no more than a "dreamer of the middle ages" (*A*, 95), spending hours among his created lords and ladies, so enrapt was he in their delicate and intricate courtly conventions. The would-be consummate craftsman caught in his own half-perfected artifice—and unfortunately, happily so. All, like Henley, have built up, projected, and imposed on themselves a certain compensating self-image, that of "the great actor with a bad part," like Salvini playing the grave-digger in *Hamlet* (*A*, 84), an image which is opposite to their real, even less heroic natures. The unconscious purpose of their restless minds is to bring life to "dramatic crisis and expression." At that high "point of artifice" and conflict between self and anti-self when the world fails their particular ideal as it must, and as they know instinctively that it must, they can at least catch a glimpse, for an extended instant, of that "true self . . . , as it were by lightning," before it finds its tongue to utter its swansong (*A*, 84). For a brief, ecstatic, and costly moment, then, they can see the antithetical halves of their natures, if not unified, then at least dramatically divided within the same vision. In this way, they can escape the representatively dismal fate of the once potentially great actress Florence Farr. Her mind should have resembled Demeter's golden sheath, but instead, because of her modern love of paradox and odd curiosities, and her modern fear and hatred of her beauty and natural talent, it became like a bundle of dry white bones from the British Museum (*A*, 81).[4] What Yeats must do is learn, repeatedly, with greater force and clarity, the lesson taught by the negative examples of these lives: not to allow the moments of visionary crisis to consume the life, nor dread of those moments to sabotage one's purpose, but rather to keep all moments in the total life process within the sphere of the imagination, for figurative enactment in one's work, and not for literal enactment—whatever the distorted form—in the world. This is the essence of tragic knowledge.

Though Yeats ironically suggests that his cook or his maid might know more about his own anti-self than he himself ever can, he nevertheless goes on, first, to specify the kind of antithesis that afflicts him and then to uncover the lineaments of his anti-self. Because nature has made him a strangely timid and self-recriminating yet still gregarious man, who goes "hither and thither looking for conversation" and who is "ready to deny from fear or favour his dearest conviction," he "loves proud and lonely things," things sufficient unto themselves, as if all in all (*A*, 115). In light of this love, which is at odds with his extremely self-conscious, Hamlet-like intellect, Yeats next begins tracing the outlines and underlining the general features of his anti-self, outlines and features which the rest of *The Trembling of the Veil* will fill in more specifically in modern terms.

From a scrap of some metrical translation of Aristophanes that he read as a boy in a local rector's library comes the fragmentary image or memory trace of the birds that sing scorn upon mankind. The next set of related images that well up come from Shelley, whom he first read as an adolescent: young sorrowful Prince Athanese, studying philosophy in some high, lonely tower. Finally, however, it is Shelley's "old man, master of all human knowledge, hidden from human sight in some shell-strewn cavern," who turns up. From *Hellas*, then, comes a favorite passage, one that Yeats recalls rang "perpetually" in his ears:

> Some feign that he is Enoch: others dream
> He was pre-Adamite, and has survived
> Cycles of generation and of ruin.
> The sage, in truth, by dreadful abstinence,
> And conquering penance of the multinous flesh,

Deep contemplation and unwearied study,
In years outstretched beyond the date of man,
May have attained to sovereignty and science
Over those strong and secret things and thoughts
Which others fear and know not.
    Mahmud. I would talk
With this old Jew.
    Hassan. Thy will is even now
Made known to him whence he dwells in a sea-
    cavern
'Mid the Demonesi, less accessible
Than thou or God! He who would question him
Must sail alone at sunset where the stream
Of ocean sleeps around those foamless isles,
When the young moon is westering as now,
And evening airs wander upon the wave;
And, when the pines of that bee-pasturing isle,
Green Erebinthus, quench the fiery shadow
Of his gilt prow within the sapphire water,
Then must the lonely helmsman cry aloud
"Ahasuerus!" and the caverns round
Will answer "Ahasuerus!" If his prayer
Be granted, a faint meteor will arise,
Lighting him over Mamora; and a wind
Will rush out of the sighing pine-forest,
And with the wind a storm of harmony
Unutterably sweet, and pilot him
Through the soft twilight to the Bosphorus:
Thence, at the hour and place and circumstance
Fit for the matter of their conference,
The Jew appears. Few dare, and few who dare
Win the desired communion. (*A*, 116)

This passage defines Yeats's lifework (as its imagery clearly informs many of his central poems): namely, to quest for the desired communion with the sage, buried within Yeats himself, who possesses, like Faust, all and so dreadful knowledge, but who has won it, unlike him, through a severe self-discipline alone. More inaccessible than God, the Wandering Jew grants an audience only to those who can in turn win the right to it by persevering in this most exacting of all quests. In the context of Yeats's then recent disappointing return with the family to London's Bedford Park, it is clear why the young man would need a model of the wise survivor: a sage, both cursed and blessed by his own awful and hard wisdom, who has lived, thereby, to wander through many "cycles of generation and of ruin," untouched and alone. Similarly, in light of his continuing and growing alienation from the crisis-ridden world, it is no wonder that, in reaction, Yeats continually celebrates the idea of "some lonely mind admitting no duty to us" as the source of all our knowledge. He ignores completely, of course, Shelley's ironical qualification: "May have attained." So strong are Yeats's need and hope. From such a universal mind, within his own personal unconscious, he desires to learn the rudiments of imaginative survival at least: "communing," as it does, "with God only, conceding nothing from fear or favour" (A, 117).

Unlike the earlier passage about Maud Gonne, which is useful for introducing the major theme and imaginative procedures in *The Trembling of the Veil*, the above passages on Yeats's central autobiographical symbols and his anti self show his peculiar meditative method in full operation. He explicitly and unapologetically describes not only events or people but "those patterns into which they fall" when he is "the looker-on" (A, 221). As he learns from Macgregor Mathers (A, 125), meditation upon the intricate configuration of a complex geometric symbol (a mandala if you will), can give rise to concrete imaginative images seemingly out of the Great Memory. These images then compose and arrange themselves into a dramatic scene according to an inherent visionary logic of their own, one not dependent solely, it appears, on association or suggestion. Significantly, when

90

Mathers first works his method on Yeats, the scene that eventually forms itself is that of a black titan in the desert raising himself up over a mound of ruins. Mathers has to tell Yeats the origin of this figure—one of the secret order of spirits in the esoteric tradition, the Salamanders. Yeats comments elsewhere in *The Autobiography* on this method. As he imagines it, vision comes only when his nature, which never ceases to judge itself and others, exhausts merely personal emotion by the rigors of carrying out that very process of judgment to its antithetical extremes. The result is that something impersonal, summoned by the spectacle of dramatic crisis, provoked in this case by the schematic conflict of Yeats's own antithetical judgments or interpretations, takes final imaginative shape and starts suddenly up into the conscious mind from the unconscious where it has been growing anonymously for some time, just as his memories of his own anti-self and its origins do here in the above passage from *The Autobiography*. This "something" is "as unforseen, as completely organized, even unique [and authoritative], as the images that pass before the mind between sleeping and waking" (*A*, 222). This "something," like Yeats's "black titan," is an image in human form that seems to grow in the rich text of the living language that constitutes the Anima Mundi.[5]

The purpose of the meditation is to discover knowledge of that self, beyond the modern ego, which lies buried under the latter's trivial, abstract, and generally narcissistic concerns. Apropos of the above example from Yeats's practice in *The Trembling of the Veil*, the stylized and intricate constellation of his friends' psyches gives rise dialectically to early personal and archetypal memory traces of that image which he learns to recognize must be that of his buried anti-self.[6] Yeats's schematizations of his friends' psyches catch and freeze them, as if at a moment of feverish crisis. This crisis is primarily Yeats's own crisis of interpretation, the one he suffers through in the formation of theirs here in his text. The result of his crisis is that, as we have just seen, the more powerful and self-convincing interpretations that arise from his unconscious and that reveal finally the lineaments of his anti-self can break through the ego's narrower views. In this way, the residue of the ego's limited interpretations of his friends, to change the metaphor, might be aesthetically burned away. Their anti-self of the tragic actor emerges from their natural self then in sharp contrast to his own: the sage of imaginative survival. In this particular way, therefore, his friends can be said to become symbolic texts, dialectically arranged, by whose antithetical light Yeats can begin to read and decode the written characters of his own "buried self:"[7]

> Ille. . . . I seek an image, not a book.
> Those men that in their writings are most wise
> Own nothing but their blind, stupified hearts,
> I call to the mysterious one who yet
> Shall walk the wet sands by the edge of the stream
> And look most like me being indeed my double,
> And prove of all imaginable things
> The most unlike, being my anti-self,
> And, standing by these characters [traced in the
>   sand] disclose
> All that I seek; and whisper it as though
> He were afraid the birds, who cry aloud
> Their momentary cries before it is dawn
> Would carry it away to blasphemous men.[8]

Against the background of cultural fragmentation ("Why should we believe that religion can never bring round its antithesis?"—A, 210) and creative decline ("every stroke of the brush exhausts the impulse"—A, 210), Yeats's subsequent immersion in nationalist-related organizations ("Ireland After Parnell") and his later helpless dithering at the

obscure crossroads of esoteric traditions ("Hodos Chameliontos") become explainable, to him at least, as self-destructive lapses from the difficult struggle to find and realize his
anti-self. His feats of organization (The National Literary
Society and The Irish Literary Society) represent then an
avoidance of composition's pains and so a succumbing to
"the chief temptation of the artist, creation without toil" (*A*,
138). Yeats's politically related activities are a slower form of
imaginative suicide than that "unmotivated self-immolation"
contemplated by Parnell when he held his mistress out over
Brighton Pier (*A*, 156).[9] The lasting symbol of such irresponsible "happiness" in self-abandonment (that "Shelley
also found when he tied a pamphlet to a fire-balloon"—*A*,
135) is, fittingly enough, a coal flaring briefly into life before
it eats a pathetic hole into the final pages of an unfinished
text, to leave there only singed margins (*A*, 151).[10]

Whether it be active self-abandonment or the passive
visionary death of George Russell and his Dublin Theosoph-
ists, Yeats must avoid politics and check any faith in them.
After Parnell's fall, A. E. and company are content to wait
passively for the saving religious vision which will transform
the world. Vision will succeed, they think, where social action failed. Totally lacking in critical discrimination, accepting
everything they "see" literally, they become therefore nothing more than mirrors revealing their own internal drift and
chaos (*A*, 167). After going through the bitter mechanical
drudgery of political and literary organization, hysteria or
despair appear as welcome refuges for the supposedly
flabby-minded. It is for this reason that Yeats comes to view
politics (in this general sense) more and more as at best "but
half-achievement, a choice of an almost easy kind of skill,
instead of that kind which is, of those not impossible, the
most difficult" (*A*, 167). With this interpretation of Russell,
we see a clear case of Yeats's laying of his own burden—
that of a tendency to passivity—wholly on another's shoul-

ders in order to fulfill his formal design and so distance himself from himself in this—to his readers—thinly disguised fashion. He condemns Russell "to a repetition of thoughts and images that have no relation to experience" because of his sinking into the blankness of the religious visionary in an age when no creed can viably work through one so that one's visions might be sharpened and clarified in opposition to the established and still living religious structure (A, 167). Clearly Yeats shares Russell's fate to a great extent. By projecting all this on Russell, Yeats can see his dread become a distinct figure and so he can take steps to alter his future.

Rather than be swayed by the flucuations of the moment, as illustrated by the fortunes of tragic political figures or of pathetic visionaries (A, 168), the austere, wise survivor must resist the urge to become either sacrificial hero or holy fool. He must keep the image of the creator, as Yeats fully discovers here in looking back on his past, always before his eyes: "Is it not certain that the Creator yawns in earthquake and thunder and other popular displays [like political riots], but toils in rounding the delicate spiral of a shell?" (A, 167). Thus Yeats uses Parnell and Russell, as well as other related and opposing figures,[11] to project a symbolically amplified interpretation of his own antithetical progress. He lays the burden of his own dangerous hysteria and passivity almost wholly on their shoulders. A typical procedure.[12] He thereby frees himself, he distances himself from himself in this thinly disguised way, so as to preserve his imagination from any further contamination following political or social failure. But he does so only in the text. In short, it is the figures of both Parnell and Russell that become his symbolic scapegoats.[13]

Despite the (now) clear example of Russell, however, Yeats recoils, in disappointment, from any kind of rational social commitment, into the intellectually isolated embrace of the Anima Mundi. In looking there for a mythological coherence, for a new sacred text of living, unifying images,

Yeats hopes to find a basis for the Unity of Culture that he failed to achieve through social means.[14] He finds instead that, whereas before abstract opinion called up abstract opinion in his troubled mind, now image calls up image "in an endless procession." He is "lost in that region a cabbalistic manuscript," shown to him by Mathers, had warned of. He is "astray upon the Path of the Chamelion, upon Hodos Chameliontos" (*A*, 181). Like his uncle, George Pollexfen, and like Mathers himself, Yeats is a helpless visionary at this point in his life (around the time of *The Wind among the Reeds*). From his "observation" that people in the Pollexfen household seem to share complementary dreams, Yeats concludes that there must be a "nationwide multiform reverie" which determines, to some perilously uncertain degree, all our apparently rational acts and judgments. As a result of his conclusion, Yeats becomes lost in a "Hades wrapped in clouds, delighting in unintelligible images" (*A*, 170), largely of his own creation:

How could I judge any scheme of education, or of social reform, when I could not measure what the different classes and occupations contribute to that invisible commerce of reverie and of sleep; and what is luxury and what necessity when a fragment of gold braid and a flower in the wallpaper may be an originating impulse to revolution or to philosophy? (*A*, 176).[15]

But by persisting in this Yeatsian version of negative capability, hanging suspended as from his rocky perch over the confluence of streams that constitute the Anima Mundi, Yeats succeeds in extricating himself from his own dangerous isolation. From an odd experiment conducted on his young pet canaries, and concluded at the site of the text,[16] he proves to his own satisfaction at least that by relying on one's strongest and deepest instincts, on the innate creative powers of the human mind, one can save oneself from oneself. In his little antithetical scientific experiment, he isolates his young birds from their mother. Will they be able to build a nest later on from inherent knowledge alone, as Henry More would suggest, or must they learn from imitation, as John Locke would argue? All their instinctive nest-building begins, in fact, when he places a little metal saucer, like the one in which they were raised, at one side of the cage, and a bundle of hair and grass at the other. Yeats allows us to infer the obvious synthesis: that the proper combination and arrangement of antithetical images can help a person tap that deepest of all creative sources and so respond with instinctive rightness (A, 181–182). For if it is true of a bird's brain, how could it be any less so for the human mind? The relation of this antithetical experiment to Yeats's antithetical interpretation of his friends should be clear: both procedures are meant to provoke the discovery of an unexpected, unforeseeable imaginative wholeness.

The longest single passage of Yeats's interpretation of creative vision follows his report of this textual discovery. In opposition to the picture of himself as a helpless visionary, and building on the results of his experiment, Yeats presents primarily for his own meditation "the greatest obstacle" to imaginative vision "he may confront without despair" (A, 183): its terrible evils of radical and complete transformation. (This is how I translate the Yeatsian phrase, "The Vision of Evil.") Only when the artist's "intellect has wrought the whole of life to drama, to crisis" (A, 183) by means of his quest for the anti-self, can that power "from beyond his mind" (A, 182), that genius in the root sense of the word, come into his mind to join, through the mediating agency of his simplifying image, the "buried self" to "the trivial daily" ego—to the subsequent ecstatic relief of the whole man (A, 183). Though in the process the artist might have to distort and manipulate even his beloved's image, as Yeats does above with Maud Gonne's, the promised result of his art is great: "the recreation of the man through that art, the birth of a new species of man" (*A*, 187).[17] Strong imaginations, then, like those of Dante and Villon for Yeats, can unite the intellectual and emotional halves of their natures so completely, in the perfect expression of their self-torturing plight and compensating visions, that "they seem to labour for their [ideal] objects, and yet desire whatever happens, being at the same instant predestinate and free, creation's very self."[18] That is, such imaginations are ironically poised between vision and despair.

Such artists as Dante and Villon can absorb even apparently random experiences into their individual imaginative quests. They can transform pain and chance into reasons for celebrating their power to will, finally, their own fates— no matter how unfortunate and unexpected. The *amor fati* of Yeats's visionary superman,[19] then, comes to oppose the murmurings of the deracinated mystic.[20] So Yeats imaginatively repeats in symbolic, textual form his descent to Hodos Chameliontos. Amid its "Hades" of "unintelligible images" (*A*, 170), he meets there this time the figures of Dante and Villon, complementary guides who save him from, respectively, the lack of intellectual discipline and the passivity he perceives afflicting both the recollected George Pollexfen and Macgregor Mathers. The wisdom that poets bring is baleful but apparently true: the artist whose work survives is one who is strong enough to sacrifice all, even himself, for and to his "self"; namely, those symbolic patterns that support and inform his art.

Yet Yeats clearly recognizes that the desire for the absolute perfection of symbolic form is the aesthetic equivalent of the ruling abstraction. Fragmentation and decline are mirrored in the arts. On the one hand, by the loss of mythological coherence, in the breakdown of Chaucer's generalized types, for example, first into the imperious central characters of

Shakespeare's plays, and then into the "split-off" elements of those characters in Romantic and subsequent poetry (*A*, 130). A progressive, divisive fall from the classical and pagan godly heights into mere reality has occurred for Yeats. On the other hand, abstraction is also reflected more recently in the drive for aesthetic purity, in the attempt to realize in language the rarified, visionary beauties suggested by Spenser's enchanted isles or Keats's dream of *Endymion*. Purification of the fragmented elements of the former myths is then a manifestation of abstraction too: that "isolation, not the distinction, of faculty from faculty, class from class" (*A*, 131), which haunts the modern age. "I think," Yeats confesses, "that the movement of our thought has more and more so separated certain images and regions of the mind, and that these images grow in beauty as they grow in sterility" (*A*, 209). Christianity has given birth to Descartes and modern science, with these awful results. Or so Yeats sees it. Quoting from Matthew Arnold with surprising approval, he concludes that it is a "morbid effort" to attempt to overcome modern fragmentation through the perfection of both the life and the work, since, in the present context, all such efforts can express only the growing abstraction (*A*, 209). But Yeats still holds out for that "unconquerable delusion" of the Aesthetes and Decadents, when he asks if he must "reverse" the cinematography of fallen history and lead men back to the "procession of the Gods" (*A*, 131) through the power of the visionary imagination. This is Yeats's "myth" for explaining both the need and the failure to overcome modern history. It accounts for his fascination with the very effort to purify the arts following Mallarmé that intellectually at least he knows must be doomed to tragic failure: "what proud man does not feel temptation strengthened from the certainty that his intellect is not deceived?" (*A*, 207).

Though intellectually aware of the truth of Arnold's proposition, Yeats nevertheless pursues the sterile object of his aesthetic desire. In the process he clearly indicates the cost of that pursuit, even while he perfects the formal expression of his awareness. He projects the disastrous results of that quest onto his friends, giving the whole syndrome the tag: art as victimage.[21] But by mastering the repetition necessary for the perfection of symbolic form he still approaches his desired goal even while he maintains his precarious mental balance. He relies, as we shall see, on the sudden unexpected influx, as if a vision, from the unconscious to order and vitalize his imagination.

Oscar Wilde is the most representative case of the artist who is a victim to his own imagination. Yeats prefigures his fate in "Four Years" when he first introduces him. He should have suspected, Yeats says, that Wilde's "fantasy was about to take a tragic turn" since both Wilde's life with his family in his elegant, white-roomed house and his success at the time in the theater composed too perfect a situation. It could only provoke the unconscious, antithetical impulse to self-destruction (A, 90). When he reappears in "The Tragic Generation," bracketed, as is the whole book, by Yeats's attendance at Ibsen's "A Doll's House" and Jarry's "Ubu Roi,"[22] Wilde has fulfilled Yeats's suspicious hindsight up to the hilt. After that infamous trial and prison, he tries to sleep as much of the day as possible, rising only in the late afternoon and spending all his evenings and nights at the Café Royal, claiming, with a great display of bravado, that he has written "the best short story in the world," which he repeats, he also claims, ritualistically to himself each day before he gets out of bed and after he takes each meal. It is as if he must learn its lesson over and over, never able to exhaust its meaning for himself (A, 190).

For Yeats, Wilde is essentially the cruelly disgraced genius, the "great comedian" in the hands of those dramatists (the authorities and their public) who understand nothing but "vulgar tragedy" (A, 190). Wilde's "parade of gloom, all that late rising, and sleeping away his life," is not insincerity, but a necessary "elaborate playing with tragedy," a defensive re-interpretation of his plight toward the comic, that "was an heroic attempt to escape from an emotion by its exaggeration" (A, 190). Victimized by his own unconscious as a result of his perfection and inflexible imposition of his projected self-image on his life, Wilde's comedy now gains in emotional resonance, tragedy awakening in him perhaps "another self," whose impersonal wit and irony is now informed by the depths of personal suffering (A, 193). Forced by his comic genius to play out his part before a hostile public, Wilde through his story almost becomes for Yeats like one of Shakespeare's great characters. They make all things, even abysmal despair and personal ruin, serve their ruling passion's goal of absolute and perfect self-expression (A, 209). Like Strozzi's portrait of a Venetian gentleman in which the whole body seems to think, such self-created "characters" escape the fate of the modern man mirrored in Sargent's portrait of President Wilson in which only the eyes weakly speak (A, 195). Wilde can be said to be analogously transformed by Yeats's portrait of his tragedy. In Yeats's excited reverie, he seems finally to achieve a brief victory over that "mere multiplication of the personality," that creation of heterogeneous masks, he identified as his own form of compensating "insincerity" (A, 189). But he becomes at last, unfortunately for the memory of the living man once possibly behind it, the one grimacing mask—the *poète maudit* incarnate: "Wilde will never lift his head again," Yeats quotes the art critic Gleeson White in mute agreement, "for he has against him all men of infamous life." Then he adds his own final, cynical comment: "When the verdict was announced the harlots in the street outside danced upon the pavement" (A, 193).

A close look now at the story which almost gives Wilde that victory over his fate not only helps to complete Yeats's portrait illustrating the cost of that decadent, "morbid effort," but also suggests important analogies with his own formal procedures in the autobiography. Yeats must recall it to himself in its original form before Wilde spoiled it, in its later published version, "with the verbal decoration of his epoch." Memory, typically, allows Yeats to appropriate it for his own:

Christ came from a white plain to a purple city, and as he passed through the first street, he heard voices overhead, and saw a young man lying drunk upon a window sill. "Why do you waste your life in drunkenness?" He said. "Lord, I was a leper and you healed me, what else can I do?" A little further through the town he saw a young man following a harlot, and said, "Why do you dissolve your soul in debauchery?" And the young man answered, "Lord, I was blind and you healed me, what else can I do?" At last in the middle of the city he saw an old man crouching, weeping upon the ground, and when he asked why he wept, the old man answered, "Lord, I was dead and you raised me into life, what else can I do but weep?" (*A*, 190)

The structure of the story is basically the ironic contrast between the wretched lives of people excluded from life by their different deprivations, arranged in an order of increasing extremity, and their even worse lives when they are restored to "full" life by Christ's "miraculous" intervention. The irony is of a radical disappointment that pervades human existence. The grandest expectations of the imagination cannot ever seem to be even partially fulfilled by our world. Yet, as we have seen, Yeats himself typically makes an imaginative virtue of a hard necessity: "The desire that is satisfied is not a great desire . . ."[23]

The story's stark and "terrible beauty" (*A*, 190) consists in its savagely funny yet poignant reversal of Christian values, in the repetitive gospel narrative style, all for the purpose of absurdly attempting to ward off Wilde's absolute despair. It is a modern antithetical parable, with Christ rather than a generalized local character as the central, unwitting figure, the ignorant agent of the progressive revelation—in this case, of the absence of a meaningful divine order. By having Christ deconstruct his own validity, the story enacts the ritual creation of an ironic symbol—the story itself, with Christ for its hollow, collapsing center of reevaluated "highest" values. The text here is then a necessary, ironic defense against the very emotion it so finely, if dialectically articulates. The health of the imagination is maintained, in such extremity as Wilde's, only by a refusal to allow oneself to be hypnotized by any single detail of our life, even one's own remorse and despair. The form Wilde's refusal takes is this savagely funny reinterpretation of his persecuting society's most fundamental cultural paradigm. Despite the danger of making the resulting work "a place of fears" (A, 210), a text on nothing more than the dubious comforts of solipsism, the modern artist, it seems, must repeat perpetually in his imaginative life the creative enactment of the imperious, yet playful words of Mallarmé's most haunting soliloquy:

> And all about me lives but in mine own
> Image, the idolatrous mirror of my pride,
> Mirroring this Herodiade diamond-eyed. (A, 214)[24]

In Yeats's transformation of his friends into autobiographical symbols, and their lives into texts for his own self-interpretation, we can see the Yeatsian adaptation of this modern strategy. At every crucial point, as in Wilde's case where he exemplifies the meaning of the title "The Tragic Generation," figures from Yeats's earlier life, already components in earlier books, reappear, acquiring added depth and greater resonance with each symbolic repetition, as if they were organic motifs in Forster's sense of rhythm in the novel. Yeats's friends, and even his own earlier "selves," become metaleptic figures.[25] They become representative allusions to entire life styles. Yeats repeatedly re-interprets these life styles, with an ever-growing and painful clarity, as nothing more than what they were predestined to be: formal elements of his autobiography. They are used to attempt to articulate, once again, an ideal, perfect text, in compensation for a failed life.[26] In this complex, ironic way, Yeats strives toward "the intellect's crowning achievement" (*A*, 252), the symbolic ordering and imaginative purification of the mind's contents, which for him is the essential goal of the religious impulse. An original and radical innocence is the imagined ideal that leads Yeats on. Like Dowson in his sadder, more vulgar way (see his hopeless love for an Italian innkeeper's lively young daughter), Yeats longs to be one of "the angels . . . who move perpetually, as Swedenborg has said, towards 'the day-spring of their youth'" (*A*, 207).[27]

But, as Yeats reveals in his antithetical analysis of Synge, he must see the creative process as the continuous, dynamic interaction of intellect and emotion, of ironic awareness and imaginative desire (*A*, 232): "No mind can engender till divided in two . . . that of a Keats or a Shelley falls into an intellectual part that follows, and a hidden emotional flying image." One may add, that of a Yeats as well.[28] This is why Wilde's final image cannot form the basis of Yeats's anti-self.

While recalling the figure of John Davidson, Yeats suddenly discovers the appropriately contrasting self-image. It is one suggested by some of the useful qualities of his friends and poetic heroes, but in the form in which it finally emerges here it seems primarily of Yeats's own unique, visionary creation. The watch-mender arises from the unconscious almost as if the image were the natural consequence of Yeats's meditative method. Its modern form is perhaps based on an observed workman, but, more importantly, its essence is defined by the spontaneously modified archetype that Yeats's antithetical craft uncovers and develops. The god-image peculiar to him appears in a reduced modern form to insure that Yeats can preserve and develop his imaginative innocence by being able to repeatedly confront the bitter complexities of his experience and feel confident that he can survive, a confidence so necessary to successful poetic creation. The quest for imaginative innocence is not in itself debilitating. It is so only for those who cannot persevere in the process of antithetical interpretation long enough to discover the god-image that is most appropriate for them and their time.[29]

John Davidson is a jealous Scot. His lack of intellectual receptivity and culture distorts his potential for poetic genius by making him anarchic and indefinite, without pose or gesture, in his response to the antinomies of experience. For our poet of the Mask, this means that he is clearly unfit for the extended rigors of composition. For example, rather than unwisely championing the idea of crude animal vigor, of "blood and guts," in obvious and extreme reaction to the admittedly anemic aesthetic of the Rhymers, Davidson should have instead been enthusiastic for the all-too-brief example of devotion to verse-craft afforded him by Dowson, Johnson, and Symons. If Davidson had paid attention, as it were, he might also have "grown a successful man" (A, 211–213), as Yeats himself did, by learning from both the limited positive example of the work and the greater, if sadder, negative example of their ruined lives:

for they had what I still lacked [as did Davidson], conscious deliberate craft, and what I must lack always [as must Davidson also], scholarship. They also taught me that violent energy, which is like a fire of straw, consumes in a few moments the nervous vitality, and is useless in the arts. Our fire must burn slowly, and we must constantly turn away to think, constantly analyse what we have done in our work, be content even to have little life outside our work, to show, perhaps, to other men, as little as the watch-mender shows, his magnifying glass caught in his screwed up eye. Only then do we learn to conserve our vitality, to keep our mind enough under control and to make our technique sufficiently flexible for expression of the emotions of life as they arise. (*A*, 212)

This image mediates between the dangers of solipsism, or the weaknesses of a too strong imagination, and the recalcitrant heterogeneity of the objective world. The poet, it suggests, must absorb reality only so much at any one time, and only very slowly, even obsessively, conserving his imaginative vitality all the while, as he works painstakingly bent over his delicate textual mechanisms. Though mechanisms, they still respond to his delicate, firm—his jeweler's—touch, as if with a life of their own. They force him to make some painful self-discoveries when their reminder of his mortality—inscribed on their faces—glitters brightly in his own eyeglass. Because Davidson never does learn, he "must hammer the cold iron," as he himself puts it to Yeats, now that his fire has consumed itself. (Shortly thereafter, lacking a god-image to guide him, Davidson predictably drowns himself.) Yeats learns, however, from this suggestive figure of the watch-mender, his god-image, that he has summoned up through his antithetical method of self-interpretation. Based on the implicit patterns of his youthful intuitions that he has been developing in the autobiography all along, it essentially tells him that he must continue to emulate the ideal of the sage or wise survivor in the form of the deliberate craftsman of the unconscious. Not the artist as unconscious victim, nor as innocent angel, nor as visionary superman, nor as Romantic hero. Instead this more sensible, somewhat ironic version of the Shelley's more grandly wise "old man." An appropriately modern image: the Creator scaled down to watch-mender size, the anonymous craftsman of tragic knowledge.

This simplifying image is what might be termed an enabling device then. Yeats can use it to organize his imaginative life around its model of a saving routine. He will nourish and conserve his creative energies thereby, essentially so that he can imagine and make the most powerful tragic and visionary poetry in the century. As long as the necessary conflict between self and anti-self, between world and word, truth and design, which feeds those energies is carried out, under the watch-mender's most scrupulous eye, then the disciplined creator's "tragic joy" need never suddenly turn into just plain despair while he is creating his discrete, dialectically related symbolic works.

In light of his textual discovery, Yeats qualified his celebration of Unity of Being, that static ideal of every faculty's perfect humming. For he sees in the idea of "the perception of change upon the instant, like the sudden blacking out of the lights of the stage," a more realistic ideal for the artistic quest.[30] Technique need not be made pure, but rather "sufficiently flexible for expression of the emotions of life as they arise." Dante's fixed image of a perfectly proportioned human body, or Yeats's father's confused notion of the simultaneous sounding of all the strings of our being, must give way to the symbol of the dancer. Unity of Being must change into Unity of Becoming.

The dancer is a familiar symbol to Yeats critics, and to scholars of the Symbolist movement as well.[31] But it is made uniquely Yeats's own in a way that needs to be spelled out in a revised form in order to meet the challenges of recent criticism. The dancer is a dialectical symbol, incorporating the ideas of both pattern and motion, in its suggestion of the harmonious creative development of those opposing mental states that arise, "diachronically," in response to that "perception of change upon the instant." As such, the dancer could not possibly be a sign of the ironic spatialization of temporal existence that Yeats has been accused of. The dancer does not stand for that aesthetic "withdrawal from ex-

106

istential time into the eternal simultaneity of essential art" that a recent critic identifies as the hallmark of modernism, generalizing too hastily from Stephen Dedalus' aesthetic of stasis in *Portrait* to include Yeats and all the rest rather indiscriminately. Though the toll of being an artist who imagines a temporal dialectic might be considered too great, the art in the "final" analysis does not then become inhuman: "We live with images, that is our renunciation."[32] The symbol of the dancer seems to be instead a constitutive ideal, the necessary human vision of the imperiled imagination in a hard time, the compensatory vision of the watch-mender's that inspires Yeats in turn to imagine his life with all the authenticity he can as the text of a play whose sequence of acts has no final end but death, and yet whose interim, hardwon "end" is nothing more than "progressive," antithetical growth in painful self-knowledge. As Yeats suggests at one especially revealing point, his art might be best figured "as some Herodiade of our theatre," only "dancing" this time "*seemingly* along in her narrow moving luminous circle" (*A*, 215; my emphasis).[33]

Not surprisingly, to pursue the ideal suggested by the symbol of the dancer is not the only course open to Yeats. As suggested by one set of visions that conclude "The Stirring of the Bones," those that deal with an astral woman, with inhumanly luminous skin, who shoots an arrow at a star, a disturbed Yeats can sink all too easily back into the irresistable embrace of an all-consuming Anima Mundi, especially once he is safely within the protective confines of Lady Gregory's estate at Coole. Yeats is convinced, even years later, that these visions heralded his fortunate meeting with his matronly but talented benefactress. As a mother would, she helps simplify his confused mind by having him collect folk tales from her peasants—the basis for *The Celtic Twilight*. With his patron's financial support and encouragement, then, Yeats does finally feel, after a long period of nervous collapse, that he can organize a National Theatre and begin to systematize and consolidate his visionary insights, so that the next generation may have something on which to build as the world at large enters its latest phase of decline. Yet the origins of these monumental visions suggest another picture. They follow his consultation of a medium for his "old trouble," which hitherto only sleeping upon a board could help curb. Similarly, his obsessive search for complementary visions among friends and associates contributes to that more unfavorable portrait. We get the impression of an almost childish visionary desperately needing the visions he must all too happily wait upon. The A. E. in Yeats looms large once again. Significantly, even the later Yeats is still too much the child as illustrated by his need to footnote these visions extensively (*A*, 247–54; 389–92).[34] So enraptured by his visions is Yeats that it is almost as though he might give up the painful composition of the work for the delightful contemplation of related but generally peripheral visions.

But another set of visions argues just as strongly against this conclusion. While recalling the impression that Maud Gonne made on him at some political rally, Yeats presents the ideal balance between vision and work in his portrait of the unpersuadable beloved. He sees in Maud an image of his art. Her beauty, backed by her great imposing stature, her commanding presence and voice, seems "that assembly's very self, fused, unified, and solitary" (*A*, 242), as if it were a significant aesthetic, even mythological achievement arising out of a people's whole tortuous experience. The living beauty of her face especially, like that of some Greek statue, shows little thought, and yet her entire body clearly seems nonetheless "a master-work of long-labouring thought, as though Scopas had measured and calculated, consorted with Egyptian sages, and mathematicians out of Babylon . . . that he might outface even Artemesia's sepulchral image with a living norm" (A, 242). Yeats reads into this grand vision of Maud Gonne the possibility for the achieved work to thrust itself up, rising like the just reawakened body "partially [and for a moment] out of the raging abstraction" (A, 242) that defines our age. As in the dream that they halved in which Maud becomes Minerva's statue and Yeats the living fire that animates its form and speaks through its piercingly blank eyes,[35] here is a central vision for his art-work. From the self-division and wars of its most exacting creator come formal perfection and an imaginative satisfaction of some limited, life-preserving kind:

> How many centuries spent
> The sedentary soul,
> In toil of measurement
> Beyond eagle and mole
> Beyond hearing and seeing
> Or Archimedes's guess,
> To raise into being
> That loveliness? (A, 243)[36]

The sedentary soul, or the childish visionary—that is the final choice.

What lay behind the tragedies of his friends' ruined genius, and how did Yeats's imagination survive? This dual question generates all the interpretive commentary in *The Trembling of the Veil*. For example, after harrowing his mind at great length trying to answer the first part of the question (A, 199–202), Yeats comes up with—typically—an image. It suggests that, though Rossetti's visionary Pre-Raphaelitism was perhaps the strongest unconscious influence on them, it was Walter Pater's more intellectual, self-conscious aestheticism that was the guiding philosophy of their tragedies. Timid, cultural late-comers all, knowing that "all subjects have long since been explored" and exhausted (*A*, 202), they grew up seeking to enjoy where they could not create. Pater made them learned and traditional by painting all inherited culture as a rich Romantic landscape full of pageantry and games where they could quest happily for those delicately poised moments of aesthetic passion. There they could safely burn with that famous hard, gem-life flame, and so, in a period of dismal decline, make the most of their passing moments and solely for those moments' sake.

But when the period of decline became the most advanced "age of transition" since the fall of the Roman Empire, the tragic, exciting dividing of forces which was so pleasurable to view in works of art became unbearable when experienced daily in the real world. The storm attending the demise of historical Christianity, its culture and its god broke with all its terrible force around the isolated individual's head. What had seemed like a lark—according to their reading of Pater's philosophy—to search out aesthetic pleasure across the gulfs of the ages, now became a scene of deadly bewilderment when they faced the violent abyss that opened right at their own feet: "It taught us to walk upon a rope, tightly stretched through serene air, and we were left to keep our feet upon a swaying rope in a storm" (*A*, 201). Almost as if in childish spite, they then led disorderly lives and sought to rediscover the themes and even the "syntax of impulsive common life," doing all things, even this last, with deliberation and labor, never, like earlier generations, with careless and prolific abandon. What once was a playful questioning of traditional values that they never intended to destroy turned into a bitterly interminable internal debate:

is it not most important to explore especially what has been long forbidden, and to do this not only with the highest moral purpose . . . but gaily, out of sheer mischief, or else sheer delight in that play of the mind? (*A*, 218)

110

Was it that we . . . lacked coherence, or did we but pursue antithesis? (*A*, 202)

Apparently the answer to the second part of that dual
question posed above is given in the systematic interpretation discovered and disclosed, bit by bit, in *The Trembling of
the Veil*. Yeats's long-developing belief in the anti-self and
its complex role in the formation and resolution of all individual crises in self-interpretation is the weird explanation
for his imaginative survival. Before the barbarisms of the
Savage God can consume all (see Garabaldi's Cipriani: "As
for me, I believe in nothing but cannon"—*A*, 246) Yeats responds by turning inward to find that self-image most opposite his natural, contaminated self, a procedure he hopes
might help him survive in a difficult time. In the process, he
transforms and develops his memory traces of himself and
his friends into exemplary symbolic texts, from which he can
dialectically discover his anti-self. That is, he experiments
imaginatively with his own life and the crisis-ridden lives of
his friends.[37] He seeks to make himself and his world into
a tragic mask and a tragic image (*A*, 127–28), so that both
might be preserved, in a form useful for him and his own
literary reputation, from fate's loveless grasp: "We *begin* to
live when we conceive life as tragedy" (*A*, 128; my emphasis).
As such, his friends might be said to become like the stylized
figures in a play by Douchenday, who act out their parts
before a black marble wall, under a marble sky, with their
defiant masks fixed nonchalantly in their drooping hands
(*A*, 233).[38]

Thus the chronic disappointment that marked Yeats's
growing awareness and self-control in *Reveries* continues
here and deepens, as his imaginative power over his world
grows, even to the point where he self-consciously embraces,
at the conclusion of the volume, the image of the world as
an alien darkness that he has found in an ancient Gnostic

111

text.[39] So great and clear is his disappointment—especially to himself. In pursuit of his essentially tragic knowledge of himself and his fate in the modern world, Yeats makes the *Autobiography* the quintessential expression of his baleful personal myth. It incorporates texts, themes, even forms of poetic organization, that centrally inform every aspect of his greatest achievement over nearly a thirty-year period.[40]. In this imperious way, Yeats constructs for himself his own shell-strewn cavern, within which he pores over old texts of himself. He hopes to discover in them, under the annotative debris of all past revisions and re-readings, and by the sheer intensity of his tireless imaginative gaze alone, the original play of interpretation—the delicate mother of pearl spritely rounding every secret track:

A poet, when he is growing old, will ask himself if he cannot keep his mask and his vision without new bitterness, new disappointment. . . . Then he will remember Wordsworth withering into eighty years, honored and empty-witted, and climb to some waste room and find, forgotten there by youth, some bitter crust.[41]

Within each book of *The Trembling of the Veil*, then, Yeats discovers the antithetical relationship between himself and his friends by disclosing those rare qualities in himself, opposed to all those of his friends, that spontaneously allowed his imagination to survive change and disappointment where theirs did not. In short, *The Trembling of the Veil* traces Yeats's unconscious quest for "the buried self" in an attempt to repeat that quest at both a deeper and more self-conscious imaginative level despite the pain of learning bitter truths about himself and his chronic, though perhaps not finally incurable, alienation from the modern world. From the friction of juxtaposed images come the fiery seeds of his simplifying image which he then must breathe into a steady, almost all-consuming life. The war, then, has become play. But at what cost, in ordinary human terms, this risky transformation?

I shall find the dark grow luminous, the void fruitful when I understand I have nothing, that the ringers in the tower have appointed for the hymen of the soul a passing bell.[42]

4

The Faltering Image

it ends, as does every good thing
on earth, by *overcoming itself.*

—Nietzsche, *On the Genealogy of Morals*

Malachi Stilt-Jack am I, whatever I learned has run wild,
. . . All metaphor, Malachi, stilts and all. A barnacle goose
Far up in the stretches of night; night splits and the dawn
          breaks loose;
I, through the terrible novelty of light, stalk on, stalk on;
Those great sea-horses bare their teeth and laugh
          at the dawn.

—Yeats, "High Talk"

I know of no more heart-rending reading
than Shakespeare: what must a man have
suffered to have such a need of being a buffon!

—Nietzsche, *Ecce Homo*

All at once, it seems, Ireland's great-landed families must
exchange their late Victorian world of fox-hunt heroics
and dinner-party elegance for a modern scene of acrid ruins
and impersonal bureaucracy. The glittering shrines of the
Anglo-Irish cultural order, and even their lush protective

demesnes, so venerable they once seemed "unchanging" (*A*, 257), become in a flash either helpless victims of the independence movement or ironic wards of the Irish Free State: "Roxborough House was burnt down during the Civil War; Coole House has passed to the Forestry department. . . . now all the Galway estates have been divided among small farmers, their great ancient trees cut down" (*A*, 257). At the beginning of "Dramatis Personae,"[1] time, working through abstract modern opinion and its hectic embodiment, revolutionary change, brutally excises or wantonly perverts all manifestations of the—for Yeats—once healthy social organism: "The innocent and the beautiful/Have no enemy but time."[2]

Edward Martyn, a blood relation of the original race of Tullyra Castle's founders, should be a most rich inheritor of the powerful's inestimable cultural abundance. But instead he is a weird mixture of Irish Catholic and continental influences, a shanty Des Esseintes who prefers abstract pattern to living form, and a simple and severe ascetical ideal to either impassioned Protestantism or visionary mysteries: "Edward Martyn, met in London, perhaps with George Moore, had seemed . . . heavy, uncouth, countrified. . . . His Degas showed the strongly-marked shoulder blades of a dancing girl, robbing her of voluptuous charm" (*A*, 257, 259). So disappointed is Yeats at the prospect of visiting this hateful and cynical aesthete in his neo-gothic monstrosity, Tullyra Castle, that he wryly predicts to Arthur Symons, then editor of the *Savoy* and his traveling companion, that they will be met, as he had been when a boy in some crudely pretentious Sligo house, by "a barefooted servant" (*A*, 257). Certainly the thirty-year-old Yeats's, as well as the older Martyn's, paradoxical motto might well be Degas's sublime presumption, intoned in the latter's waiting ear: "Cynicism is the only sublimity" (*A*, 259).

Suddenly, before his prediction can die on his lips, Yeats

has his expectations, as usual, ironically fulfilled—but this time marvellously so: "Then I saw the great trees, then the grey wall of the Castle" (*A*, 257). The tone is surprisingly that of the awe-struck Pre-Raphaelite adolescent, his medieval dream apparently long buried under defensive irony. Similarly, when Yeats sits night after night in the great shadowy intimacy of Martyn's barely lit Gothic hall, he comes to see his host in a different light: now as a sadly self-torturing figure, "as though upon a stage set for *Parsifal* . . . his harmonium, so placed among the pillars that it seemed some ancient instrument" (*A*, 258). What Yeats calls here the man of letters' extraordinary capacity for "make-believe" (*A*, 257) saves Martyn and his haunt—and Yeats himself as well—from chronic cynicism's ultimately mummifying sublimity.

These contrasting sets of radical perspectual transitions do not merely suggest that antithetical thinking, in the form of those famous interpenetrating cones or gyres, pervades Yeats's every vision, but also that his own text is enacting, in a specially defined ironic sense, time's destructive work of instantaneous-seeming change. Within the span of a few sentences, there is a telescoping of recent and more distant moments, those of the twenties with those of the turn of the century, all overviewed by the poet writing in 1934. The young man's bitter transition from a closed and perhaps stifling old world to a wide-open and chronically alienating new one is marked by the grim precision and taut mockery of the later, more experienced and so necessarily defensive poet. (Instead of Coole House being passed on to some legitimate inheritor, it is passed ironically to the Forestry department, as if the whole affair were merely a routine office matter.) So, too, the young man's fledgling cynicism stands at least partially ruined, its awkward scavenger's wings having been quickly clipped, thanks to that flickering vision of great trees and gray Castle wall, and also that later medieval-rich shadowy atmosphere. In both cases a sterile, coercive order,

117

whether social or personal, whether a great tradition or a mean habit, breaks down under the sudden impact of the unexpected and overpowering vision that time's workings afford. Such a vision opens the temporal horizons not only to reductive nightmare but also to greater imaginative, even mythic possibilities. Most importantly, it trains Yeats's creative attention on to his own imagination, his own power of "make-believe," rather than allowing it to remain locked into defensive orders, however grandly or cleverly seen. And this is so for the remembering poet as well as the remembered man: "Then I saw the great trees, then the grey wall of the Castle."

Increasingly, Yeats's world becomes the space in which his many conflicting temporal perspectives interact in the ironic present of the text, with the result that they become ghostly presences there, ever ready to re-assume flesh and blood the moment the proper stimulus of radically antithetical patterns of interpretive interaction "allow" them to. As in Martyn's case, and also generally against the larger historical background of levelling modern divisions, a repressed fragment of an earlier perspective unpredictably starts up, returns, repeats and elaborates itself, for both the later recollecting poet and the recorded man. Such fragments are memory traces of an original innocence, a radical openness on the part of the creator in Yeats to his own imaginative history. Out of what Yeats comes to call "the tradition of myself" (A, 312),[3] such kernel texts irrupt into his life meditation to be symbolically amplified, so that the sterility of both habitual defense and blind idealizations are exposed, as more imaginative possibilities are inspired. As with Yeats's meditation on his childhood unhappiness and the ruined friends of his young manhood, the antithetical relationship here between the symbolic design of his interpretation and the remembered details of his life also provokes the discovery of a central image suggestive of the creator's perpetual in-

118

nocence, his surprising ability to confer a vital meaning on the most unlikely of scenes and figures, as witness his sudden investiture of Martyn with unexpected significance.

The focus of Yeats's interest in *Dramatis Personae* is now explicitly the violent antithesis between tradition and modernity. Since he has found his anti-self, his simplifying image of the watch-mender, and has realized he can become like him only by imitating—ultimately without energy-draining regret—his passionate craftsmanship, his painful acts of imaginative self-composition, Yeats turns his attention here to the larger social and cultural order, the tradition, he thinks is needed to preserve and transmit without perversion his imaginative bequest. Lacking a traditionally heroic order, however hypocritical and undemocratic, Yeats is now almost totally bereft of the grand themes, the living examples of great personalities that, in justifying human suffering, in making it meaningful by their grand style of existence, inspire all life's celebration in supreme art and song. Yeats, therefore, tries to construct in *Dramatis Personae*, with the help of his dramatic antithetical method, a compensating ideal paradigm of tradition: his own unique "family romance."[4] The paradigm has at its center the impossible images of Lady Gregory, Count Florimond De Basterot, Richard Gregory (the late eighteenth- and early nineteenth-century figure), and John Synge; and on its apparent periphery the opposing (and self-opposing) images of Edward Martyn and George Moore, that "peasant saint" and "peasant sinner" (*A*, 269).[5] As we shall see, however, Yeats's text, doing more of time's "destructive" work in the special double-edged sense described above,[6] razes his monumental idealizations of the Ascendancy, as well as his silly aristocratic flourishes, even as he is articulating them. It does so in the service of an ever greater irony of repeated innocence, an innocence preserved and cultivated by even more fertile imaginative or mythic fictions: Yeats's "make-believe."[7] That Yeats must learn this last hard lesson of laborious creation from the life texts of himself constitutes for him the irony of tradition, an irony which his technique, his method, does indeed discover for him, but which at the same time cannot lead to a pre-determined balance of opposing viewpoints. Instead, unlike new critical contextual irony, Yeats's textual irony leads to an openness before all viewpoints, including the comic ab-sence of all balance that defines the irrepressible child's vision.

Irony is as protean a concept as George Moore is a per-sonality, and with as checkered a career. In the Yeatsian con-text, it is not simply "an awareness of life as being funda-mentally and inescapably at odds with the world at large,"[8] but rather a phenomenon arising from the creative interac-tion of heterogeneous temporal perspectives embedded in a tradition of texts, a phenomenon, moreover, that leads to the discovery of greater imaginative possibilities for life rather than deeper alienation from one's self or one's world. The mechanism for effecting this discovery is the subtle al-teration in our view of earlier and later perspectives condi-tioned by the tradition of texts. But unlike Eliot's version of the larger cultural tradition, this tradition of texts creates no "timeless ideal order," but instead depends upon the con-stant possibility of change, of becoming, of man's funda-mental temporality breaking into our experience of reading. Such irony, the irony of tradition, demands our full engage-ment in the intellectual warfare by which each generation is appropriated and from which each tries to appropriate for itself a view that it can voice, can make, its own.

Perhaps the reader stimulated by such vigorously ironic "wrestlings" staged by Yeats's tradition of himself can begin to discern and trace in his own interpretations of those events, his own tradition of interpretive texts, the shifting image of a finer if more perplexing, even enigmatic, inher-itance than that of our generally enfeebled or prostituted

120

cultural traditions. Now, of course, all social, literary, and personal "myths" of continuity, of identity, are broken in fragments. They seem no better than the discredited "artificially created illusions" of Yeats's appropriately hypothetical and disreputable modern god, that "invisible hypnotist" of his (*A*, 326).[9] Amid the distorting welter of all our ruined culture's "original texts" there just may be comically reflected, as there is here in Yeats's life myth, *The Autobiography*, traces of the creator's first smile.

Yeats launches his project to give Ireland a national theater, and her future generations the noble memory—at least—of a living drama, within Count Florimond De Basterot's tiny garden, under his and Lady Gregory's encouraging and clearly parental eyes, and after invoking the spirit of his ideal inheritor, Richard Gregory. Gregory, neither sterile aesthete nor compromised, like Martyn, by his parents' original difference in class and religion, cuts a brilliant unconventional figure. Passionate and unpredictable to the end, he resigns his commission in the King's Guards, reputedly for honor's sake, after being acquitted of the false charge of cowardice. He then blithely carries off his beloved (but unfortunately middle-class) schoolgirl, and eventually marries her when his disapproving father dies. He squanders large sums and great amounts of energy on the Coole library and estate, carving out around the house those long sweeping avenues Yeats loves, and planting many new woods in the Coole demesne. The last of these he names—conventionally enough—after his wife, Isabella (*A*, 260). Whereas Martyn is the Irish aesthete, incarnation of the age's decline into abstraction ("his mind was a fleshless skeleton"—*A*, 260), Gregory is the dashing Romantic hero—as if out of Yeats's own adolescent daydreams over Keats, or even Lamb's Shakespeare. Gregory's exemplary spirit, Yeats likes to think, still resides within Coole House, and can be induced, as it were, to take up residence, even permanent residence, within his own works—for posterity's as well as his own benefit: "and have I not sung in describing guests at Coole—'There one that ruffled in a manly pose, for all his timid heart'—that one myself?" (*A*, 307).

Lady Gregory and Count De Basterot are the appropriately aristocratic authority figures, who, along with Yeats as the laboring, dutiful son and George Moore as the renegade, adopted son, constitute the odd makeshift family of modern inheritors that, in Yeats's recollecting eyes, must administer the tradition, preserving and recreating for our own and later ages Gregory's noble spirit. Lady Gregory is for Yeats the heroic wife of Ireland's late ambassador to Ceylon. In his eyes, she becomes a possible descendent of Shakespeare's Percy. She is a study in "feudal responsibility" because of her passion for house and country and surely not an illustration of "Victorian earnestness" that a superficial observer at first may see her as being. Lady Gregory exemplifies in her life the antithetical artist's daily choice, "a choice constantly renewed in solitude" (*A*, 264). She chooses, like the artist, to bear only those burdens laid on her by her own character and status and not any imposed from outside by impersonal authority or abstract modern opinion. She becomes, because of this choice, not only a balancer of all extremes, the ideal "center of peace" to which the disorderly modern artist naturally gravitates, but also Yeats's trusted advisor, his patron and guide,[10] that living embodiment of the "Aristotelian motto": "To think like a wise man but to express oneself like the common people" (*A*, 264). She even becomes, thanks again to this magical choice, that most unlikely thing, an antithetical artist in her own right: "Lady Gregory, in her life much artifice, in her nature much pride, was born to see the glory of the world in a peasant's mirror" (*A*, 307). Count De Basterot, that other, less important lifegiver for Yeats's increasingly more aristocratically drawn

anti-self, is an old disestablished landlord of French extrac-
tion, with a checkered past. He is, nevertheless, because of
his decision to support the Abbey project, and his loyal
friendship to Lady Gregory, still worthy of the designation
noble. He is a generalized, affectionate father figure to
Yeats's indecisive but ultimately responsible son. In this way
he balances Lady Gregory's role of determined mamma.[11]
De Basterot is the late incarnation of a favorite old Yeatsian
saying: "Things reveal themselves passing away" (A, 266).[12]

George Moore, on the other hand, is for Yeats the un-
faithful, unreliable "natural" offspring, a protean rascal serv-
ing as an imaginative sibling rival.[13] "Violent, coarse, dis-
cordant," like "a wild pendulum," he is the perfect
embodiment of the purely natural man in a fragmented time,
an impossible chaos of irreconcilable qualities. He is both
"A man carved out of a turnip, looking out of astonished
eyes" (A, 271), and a snake in Yeats's garden of tradition
shaped out of a lumpy man, "insinuating, upflowing, cir-
culative, curvicular, pop-eyed" (A, 283). Moore, secretly
closed and condemning, and Yeats "open" and "sympathetic," are "opposites," like Blake's spectre and artist. The
one, a potential "master of construction," ruthlessly sacrifices all to one central idea; the other, a connoisseur of words,
needs Moore's advice on dramatic construction and theater
direction.[14] "Like Milton's lion rising up, pawing out of the
earth," Moore strains to achieve "the discipline of style."
This is the ordering of one's words not according to logic,
but rather according to an organic hierarchy of imaginative
values. As such, it is the tradition's hallmark. Yet Moore,
"unlike that lion," gets "stuck halfway" (A, 271) in the
artist's learning process. Only before the great masterpieces
of painting would his boisterous chaos be struck dumb, if
not sensitive, by the presence of the greater culture's imposing silence. He is for Yeats a medieval ghost using the
dust and vapor, the dirty scraps of the modern world (his

naturalistic novelist phase), to fabricate a body of work for himself. Thus Moore, unlike Yeats who creates living forms, is condemned to chronic abstraction: "Because his mind was argumentative, abstract, diagrammatic, mine sensuous, concrete, rhythmical, we argued about words" (*A*, 291). The saving antithetical, formulaic argument, it seems.

As in the case of his other autobiographical symbols (see, for example, his grandfather and Dowden in *Reveries*, or Wilde and Davidson in *The Trembling of the Veil*), Yeats is projecting onto these figures in "Dramatis Personae" either hopelessly ideal qualities belied by his own text or many of his own latent tendencies that he instinctively recognizes as dangerous threats to his imaginative coherence. Whereas Richard Gregory, for example, is too much like the classic unscrupulous rake of eighteenth-century coinage (Wickham from *Pride and Prejudice* springs to mind), a generalized, distanced figure out of romantic tales and family legends, Martyn, however disagreeable a creature, is most definitely if difficultly alive. A Catholic aristocrat whose "countrified" manner makes his strange combination of ascetic and aesthetic ideals all the more strange, is just too real even for the most elaborate fiction.[15] Furthermore, Gregory, ironically enough, unthinkingly effects, and Yeats likewise celebrates, the kind of "destructive union between two traditions (*A*, 259) that earns Martyn, as the product of such a union (noble and peasant in his case), nothing but scorn. And as Gregory's lustrous unconventionality dims, Yeats's partial identification with Martyn grows clearer. They both share, for example, the artist's cruelty towards oneself ("What drove him . . . what secret torture?"—*A*, 259). Even more importantly, they both possess a compensatory fascination for abstract patterns and an original dread of the sensual flux: "The Utamaro . . . pleased him [Martyn] because of its almost abstract pattern, or because the beautiful women portrayed do not stir our Western senses" (*A*, 259). From the tone, diction, and emphasis, from the language of Yeats's interpretive contrast of these two figures, it becomes apparent that the conscious repetition of his identification with the Romantic hero (not seen fully enacted since *Reveries* where old William Pollexfen stalked the Sligo scene) is open to the ironic qualification inherent in Yeats's own "tradition of myself." In effect, Yeats is of the devil's party without really knowing it. Despite the difference between Martyn's image and Yeats's anti-self of the watch-mender there is more of a family resemblance there, as the text uncovers, than between Gregory's unquestionably dashing and dated image and that "'. . . one that ruffled in a manly pose, for all his timid heart'—that one myself." Idle dreams, even when recognized as such, are still idling.[16]

That Yeats needs to give Lady Gregory a fabulous ancestry,[17] must begin her portrait with a denial that she is a study in Victorian earnestness, and finally feels compelled to manufacture from his own later theories her amazing antithetical choice—all these necessary interpretive strategies argue not only for the ironic qualification but also for the natural ambivalent defensiveness of his idealization.[18] For all her good works, Yeats must confess, for instance, that she takes an odd calculating view of artists: "We were all like packets of herbs, each with its special quality" (*A*, 273)—apparently for her to mix, at her own discretion, into the Irish cauldron. Similarly, Yeats seems to recognize—at least implicitly—that, though she is both emotionally and financially supportive during his mid-life crisis of identity,[19] she is at the same time, of course, necessarily acting too much like the mother, if he is to have any hope left of becoming autonomous. That is, she makes him dependent. This recognition is not simply a product of the later poet's reflection on the early man's troubles, "ought I to *let* you do all these kind things for me" (*A*, 273; my emphasis), Yeats asks in a passage quoted here from a letter of that time. The unspoken answer, appropriately, would be another question: Do you have or want to have the choice.[20]

In the same way, Yeats's own text opens De Basterot's ghostly father's role to opposing—in this instance comic—possibilities. His heroic endurance of his many losses consists in taking sympathetic friends on nostalgic tours of his former holdings, and pointing out to them where there "had once been park, where the garden walls had stood" (A, 265). His death, the climactic symbolic revelation of his supposedly noble essence, is, likewise, almost funny. For after Yeats pronounces his old saying, "Things reveal themselves, passing away," it seems De Basterot can not then pass away soon enough: "We never saw him again" (A, 266). Finally, when Yeats quotes the obituary notice, with all its pretensions to a now hopelessly lost grandeur, the resulting incongruity between the all-too-apparent and pathetic "reality" and the consciously concocted and grandiloquent "myth" is too great, too absurd, for solemnity:

In five or six weeks several men and women with old titles announced upon a black-edged card the death of "Florimond, Alfred, Jacques, Comte de Basterot, chevalier de l' Ordre du Saint Sepulchre, leur Cousin Germain, et Cousin . . ." (A, 266)

This passage could have been taken, without substantial change, from a Beckett work: "chevalier de l'Ordre du Saint Sepulchre"? Only where Beckett of course hits, Yeats here clearly is the mark.

Yeats's version of George Moore is an especially striking example of the text, as it were, undermining itself. But whereas the interpretations of the aristocrats either self-destruct in isolation, or, apropos of Martyn and Gregory, cancel themselves out in relation to one another, Yeats's view of Moore represents instead the possibility of his own interpretive blindness overcoming itself. Since Yeats's interpretation is here the most extremely critical, it can paradoxically be read as a defensive cover that, once removed, will expose Yeats's own innocence of becoming in the difficult making.[21] Yeats himself, as we have seen, is like Moore, a living chaos, a bundle of heterogeneous texts, familial, literary, and collective, that must be ordered under the sign of his discovered simplifying image by his creative imitation of the watch-mender. So, too, his own wild pendulum swings (now the Celtic Twilight, now Renaissance Italy, now Maud Gonne, now Iseult, her daughter) are notorious. Yeats's own vacillations may seem less disorderly than Moore's not only because it is Yeats who is doing the interpreting here, but also because Yeats has made his vacillations form a pattern of literary development in the corpus of his works. That he has done so does not, however, argue for his radical difference from Moore, even if one grants that Moore's own work does not also show any comparable achievement. For Yeats only struck the casting of his development by first melting down, through his defensive projections, all his friends, that is, all his own disguised negative features that he saw in his friends. Furthermore, the violence, discordance, and crudity (if not coarseness) of Yeats's deeds of interpretation belie all his claims to being genuinely open and forgiving, as well as revealing his essential likeness to the Moore he portrays. Yeats instinctively sees Moore as that natural self within him that he has been struggling against by his pursuit of the anti-self. For example, Yeats claims: "I have read no book of his, nor would I, had he not insisted, for my sympathies were narrow—I cared for nothing but poetry and prose that shared its intensity" (A, 272). Notice how Yeats artfully confesses to a special kind of narrowness of taste only to subtly charge Moore and his work with a less endearing kind, almost with a voluptuous miserliness. This is especially ironic since Moore is supposed to care only for construction and nothing for words at this time in his career. Yeats seems more like the harsh, unsympathetic judge than his alleged spectre ever does, despite the latter's sudden, crude outbursts and vulgar reprisals. (He publicly kicks, for example, a recalcitrant lover in the behind—provoking Yeats's private envious amusement as well as his formal expression of distaste).[22] But most tellingly, it is that perfectly antithetical formulation of their essential difference that forges the final link of identity, for it is itself, of course, a very fine example of Yeats's own "argumentative, abstract, diagrammatic" habit of mind—a habit central to the composition of *The Autobiography*. That Yeats also claims sensitivity to words, to style, in this same formulation can only appear, to his great disadvantage of course, highly ironical. Perhaps it is Yeats himself, rather than Moore, who is that medieval ghost "making a body for itself" not out of the modern world's "drifting dust and vapour," but out of the figures—either exemplary or scapegoat—at the interpretive center of his life text.

As all the applications of mottoes, proverbs, quotations, and formulaic descriptions attest, Yeats's friends and associates function for him as formal illustrations of various psychological and intellectual principles, rhetorical figures with symbolic or abstract significances, that are part of explicit and implicit antithetical arguments. The ultimate effect of the reader's recognition that Yeats's friends are symbolic elements in an ironic text is not, however, simply the invalidation of his conscious intentions and idealized or uncritical interpretations in favor of his denigrated figures. Nor is it to balance or cancel out both sets of figures. Rather it is, in Moore's case especially, to make us see them as—however perversely—inspired. Yeats's own energetic, impassioned, and detailed critique of Moore allows him to become in a subtle and clearly dialectical way a lively, interesting, sympathetic, if still coarse character. With each appearance throughout the middle sections of "Dramatis Personae" (Lady Gregory dominates the opening and closing sec-

128

tions),[23] Moore gains in solidity, despite his figural nature, even as his many metamorphoses are enacted under our eyes. Naturalistic novelist, aesthete, rake, reformed sinner, country gentleman, arch obsessive stylist—he becomes them all. He is an energetic protean role player. Thus Yeats's own harsh interpretation of Moore not only reflects back as harshly on himself (who else is more the role player than Yeats?), but it also sheds a kinder light on this vital devil. In the process it restores this strange man's innocence of becoming. Under this and Yeats's other interpretations must lie, partially disclosed, partially hidden, many antithetical imaginative possibilities, all those of his own distorted self-image: "Like Milton's lion rising up, pawing out of the earth, but unlike that lion, stuck halfway" (A, 277).

Yeats's text is, as we have seen, like those "shut-in mysterious places" from his childhood where one plays and waits for something marvellous to happen. In *Reveries* and *The Trembling of the Veil* Yeats focuses and imposes his abstract antithetical patterns of interpretation (a method of contemplation, as we have seen, learned from Mathers), on the traces or primal texts of various autobiographical symbols. He then waits for the complex, particular, often mythic world of his discovered interpretation to generate and symbolically articulate itself:

He gave me a geometrical cardboard symbol and I closed my eyes. Sight came slowly, there was not that sudden miracle as if the darkness had been cut with a knife, . . . but there rose before me mental images that I could not control: a desert and black Titan raising himself up by his two hands from the middle of a heap of ancient ruins (A, 125)

At the center of such elaborated or repeated texts he hopes to witness, as if all creation's secrets suddenly rose before him, the slow, spontaneous realization of his anti-self. The text for Yeats, then, is a compositional phenomenon or process in the strictest psychological sense: "It is myself that I remake." Yeats's autobiographical method, rudimentary in *Reveries*, perfected in *The Trembling of the Veil*, becomes in *Dramatis Personae* nearly autonomous. When employed consciously for other than the fulfillment of his inescapable antithetical quest, that is, for the construction of a consoling and defensive family romance of a narrowly based aristocratic tradition, the text itself then deconstructs the ideal Anglo-Irish dream, turns against itself, not just to allow George Moore his unexpected innocence, but also to make possible the imaginative context in which Yeats can learn his last lesson. Blind idealization, like cynicism, or any other mechanism of defense, can never be sublime for the authentic creator—or even for the would-be aristocrat of creation.

At first Yeats seems hopelessly dependent on that bearer of the Anglo-Irish tradition, Lady Gregory. But then he gradually becomes more independent, hoarding resentment for George Moore because—one of many reasons—he must even temporarily rely on him for advice on stage direction and dramatic construction. Finally at the conclusion of "Dramatis Personae" Yeats stands vacillating between familiar alternatives: between an all-embracing but also all-consuming vision and the self-dividing but also ecstatic creative work. As in the visions of the Coole Archer found at the end of *The Trembling of the Veil*, here, too, Lady Gregory is the vision's vehicle: "Sleep a little, sleep a little, for there is nothing at all to fear, Diarmuid, grandson of Duibhne . . . to whom I have given my love" (*A*, 307). Yeats finds in her "inspired" translations of tales from Ireland's heroic past the appropriately ideal repose from the labors of his dramatic creation. Repeating such a vision here, and at such length (*A*, 307–8), is a consolation for his later efforts, in recollecting this period in his life, to construct his private paradigm of the modern Irish tradition. Yet he also as clearly still feels the need to perfect himself by realizing not the aristocratic poseur but the authentic anti-self of the watch-mender, a need also disclosed by the repetition of such passages as the following: "When I wrote verse, five or six lines in two or three laborious hours were a day's work, and I longed for somebody to interrupt me" (A, 295). This is a far cry from the life-long goal of his labors:

> all hatred driven hence,
> The soul recovers radical innocence
> And learns at last that it is self-delighting,
> Self-appeasing, self-affrighting,
> And that its own sweet will is Heaven's will.[24]

And this is why he becomes a man who must seek out, even years later, the example of men who have "style." These men—all idealized paternal figures—are mimics, as it were, of his own perfect autonomy. He must emulate them in the creation of his work if he is to overcome his timid heart— not so he can pose heroically but so he can face the tortures of composition and enact in his work his own truths no matter how terrible or demeaning they may be. The all-enabling old man must permanently replace the all-consuming old woman.

The play of interpretation does not now, as perhaps might automatically be expected, simply present such an exemplar of style to be dismantled almost in the same breath, nor does it contrast one figure with another, with the apparently disapproved figure turning out to be the one Yeats secretly identifies with. Neither simplistic nor predictable, the play of interpretation is ever-growing and changing. It proceeds from single passages, through closely related scenes, to different portions of the same volume—or even of separate volumes. In Standish O'Grady and William Fay (the actor), Yeats sees complementary examples of what it means to have style: that original self-possession. O'Grady in *The Trembling of the Veil* is the archetype of the Irish writer who must sing a swan song of rage for all that has been lost of the ruling culture. Now in "Dramatis Personae" he is an Ascendancy inheritor who, unlike most others, can still focus his "heritary passion" (*A*, 280). That is, he reappears, subtly changed, as the essential man, as the man wholly and nobly himself, the heroic articulator, despite all circumstances or personal consequences, of unpopular stands. Having style means he can rise above the "all-too-human" by means of his forceful, logical, and imaginative use of words, through the pure clear power of his organic dialectic: "this man had it [style] . . . When in later years compelled to answer some bitter personal attack, he showed that alone among our public men he could rise above bitterness, use words that, for all their convincing logic, made his reader murmur" (*A*, 284).

Yeats sees in Fay, on the other hand, not only a reason for hoping he could some day hear "Greek tragedy spoken with a Dublin accent" (*A*, 301), but also a complex, well-rounded, more innocent if still noble figure. All the twists and turns of interpretation, typically enough, have stimulated such a discovery: "He could play dirty tramp, stupid country man, legendary fool, insist on dirt and imbecility; yet play—paradox of the stage—with indescribable personal distinction" (*A*, 303). An acceptably distanced and "stylish" George Moore, it seems, can be safely celebrated. Clearly O'Grady and Fay become Yeats's models for the ideal synthesis of logic and imagination, of passion and control, nobleness and play that he calls "style." He must try to imitate them as he did their less successful, more confusing than enlightening prototypes like William Pollexfen, by imaginatively incorporating and ordering their qualities in his own work. To choose between the vision and the work, to choose finally what he terms the modern creator's "perpetual, painful, purification" (A, 293),[25] demands that he look to such men who, in their different ways, transcend their own bitter complexities through the power of their literary and dramatic imaginations to open themselves to their best selves, even as they are exposed in their life or profession to all the threatening signs of fragmentation and decline: "[they] alone . . . could . . . use words . . . that made their reader [and listener] murmur."

Varieties of meditation on style, personal, literary, imaginative, with the figure of John Synge as a focus—this could be a description of the extracts from Yeats's diary kept in 1909 that make up *Estrangement* and *The Death of Synge*. Though written long before "Dramatis Personae," they nevertheless bear—in their selected and re-arranged form[26]— on Yeats's need to shape his own style for later life. Even apparently random aphoristic extracts reveal Yeats's obsession: "My father says a man does not love a woman because he thinks her clever or because he admires her, but because he likes the way she has of scratching her head" (A, 313). Furthermore, the opening two notes of *Estrangement* not only announce the theme ("Style, personality—deliberately adopted and therefore a mask—is the only escape from the hot-faced bargainers and the money-changers"—A, 311), but also show Yeats experimenting with his antithetical method of self-interpretation. For, on the one hand, they decry the logic of books where one thing must lead to another as part of an insidious "surrender to literature," which must be avoided at all costs if the sense of life, of imaginative strength, like Jesus' or Buddha's, is to be preserved and developed; while, on the other, they enact just such a logical, literary progression. This apparent contradiction between form and content is actually a necessary, perhaps unsuccessful, experiment in applying his antithetical method to the obsessions of his own mind in the hope that an authentic

Yeatsian mask may be discovered and then consciously adopted.[27] In pursuit of his anti-self Yeats elaborates in these notes a core of self-interpretation that, clearly Nietzschean,[28] establishes the foundations of his later more fully developed autobiographical standpoint, for which Synge is here the "ur-text."

Since the Renaissance, it seems, man more and more has come to be seen as an isolated "individual fact," captive of his "limiting environment" or some mechanical "idiosyncrasy" (A, 339). Modern science, the essence of the Counter-Renaissance and the natural antithesis created out of the Christian religion has inspired all those intellectual and literary movements, like naturalism, which embody this disillusioned and cynical view of man. This life-negating view is at the heart of "the anarchic revolt of individualism." This revolt is really a revolt of the masses of unformed and deformed modern egos, the ego being a ghost of the Christian soul, that original distorted image of the body's power. In such a context, man is seen at best as a passive "mirror" of aesthetic delights, never a burning brazier" (A, 323), and at worst, never as a lean hard Stoic, but rather as a delicate "flower" ready to condemn all life if he cannot savor his exquisite Pateresque moments in peace, free from all protracted, painful struggle: that is, abstracted from the very conditions of all life. What has happened, Yeats believes, is that Christianity has passed off "a spurious copy" of the heroic Classical tradition, that inspiration of the Renaissance. Time and again, under different perverting guises the life-affirming, art-inspiring heroic truths have been passed to each generation until with Arnold they become so "formal" and "empty" that they are "a vulgarity"—or, even worse, a subject to be studied and appreciated like the "Classical forms passed from Raphael to the Academicians" (A, 332–33). From man as the heroic measure of all noble things; through man as an alien soul whose perverse moral values life can never measure up to; to the notion that all men are just things to be measured by a mean calculative ego—such is Yeats's view of the progressive decline of the West. So sedimented is this mean interpretation of life that it is often not even recognized as an interpretation at all, let alone one that needs re-evaluation.

According to Yeats, the modern artist, inheriting this situation, should not give in to passive self-critical reflection or sterile defensiveness. Instead, he must imitate in the creation of his works the active, even aggressive heroic models of a Christ or Caesar.[29] Out of the artist's tradition of himself, out of all his created life texts, "a secondary or interior personality," an anti-self, will then begin to take form. Only from the long self-torturing conflict between self and anti-self may the artist "come face to face" with what is "permanent in the world," all the authentic feelings of ever greater life and imaginative power, and so become, his will stimulated and tested to the utmost, a creative fire, an impersonal "energy that hates everything that is not itself" (A, 337).

The artist thus becomes suddenly the creator, almost a god or daimon, whose greater, archetypal mind, "like an overflowing well" (A, 319), seems "immeasurably bold—all is possible to it" (A, 322). Confronted by tragedy, by the final destruction of all he holds dear, such a man never despairs, but is possessed instead by that "joy . . . which is the other side of sorrow" (A, 338), that greater "egotism of the man of genius" Synge had, "which Nietzsche compares to the egotism of a woman with child" (A, 346). Fragmentation, destruction, therefore, is not alien to the creator in the man, but is the essential element out of which this transmuter of everything not himself makes antithetical images of himself and his world. Like Synge again, the creator is "completely absorbed in his own dream," not simply for the dream's sake, nor for the dreaming, so much as for his own "exhaustive

135

contemplation" (A, 338) of life's greater and healthier imaginative possibilities, of which he himself is the irreplaceable
exemplary source: "It was as though we and the things about
us died away from Synge and not he from us" (A, 346).[30]

Thus, despite the growing ruin, the accelerating collapse
of all centers of value in the "spurious" Western tradition,
Yeats hopes to become, like Synge, the perpetually innocent
creator of his own world, not to escape any other, but to
nourish his—and our—power to grow even more imaginatively, more emphatically alive. Yeats, in sum, wants to
become a lover of his own fate, however horrible (since "all
external events" are but "an externalization of character").
To become consciously, willfully, the self one can unthinkingly be before crisis, with all one's original childlike self-
possession still intact: this is the ultimate text of the would-
be creator. For the energetic celebrant of irrepressible life, it
is the text of symbolic repetition which he faces in the creation of his antithetical imaginative works: "I think all happiness depends on the energy to assume the mask of some
other self; that all joyous or creative life is the re-birth as
something not oneself; something which has no memory and
is created in a moment and perpetually renewed" (A, 340).
This "something not oneself" (Yeats often uses "self" to
mean "ego" and "anti-self" to mean what I mean by
"self,")[31] is that other personality the artist has instinctively
become in the past when he has spontaneously acted out in
the world those essentially symbolic and often destructive
crises of self-definition which must be imaginatively enacted
in the work if his creative innocence is to survive. Symbolic
repetition is the fruit of the creator's life: all that he latently
is becomes the imaginative text of himself that he finally wills
to be.

Coming as it does after Yeats's idealization of the Ascendancy and his own aristocratic posturings, such an original Nietzschean core of interpretation behind the develop-

ment of *The Autobiography* suggests that perhaps O'Grady alone must be Yeats's exemplum of heroic style for later life. And yet such a conclusion, though obviously possible, would be too hasty, too easy. For one thing, despite its heroic trappings, the Ascendancy is part of the larger Western tradition, that "spurious copy" of the authentic tradition. Its origins are ultimately those of the Counter-Renaissance, the Reformation, capitalism, modern science. Furthermore, Yeats's view of the mask, of style, suggests not simply the creator's need to appear like O'Grady, but his ability to be different from all his poses so as to develop his power to become any one of them at his imaginative will: "Some day setting out to find self knowledge, like some pilgrim to the Holy Land, the artist will become the most romantic of characters. He will play with all masks" (*A*, 327). Finally, given Yeats's ingrained dialectical habit of mind, his later choice of a tradition, ironically enough, may ultimately be no more than the conscious creation of a fiction necessary to preserve the creator's imaginative innocence, to test his powers of concentration, his will to sustain, like Synge, a complete absorption in his own dream whatever the distractions or the dream. In short, for the strong stimulation of every faculty it affords, the constant crises of interpretation it provokes: "for the general purposes of life you must have a complex mass of images, something like an architect's model" (*A*, 334–35). Such "fictions," like Yeats's gyres, for example, are not merely personal conventions. For they are imaginatively compelling while the artist is under their influence. Rather they are more like Jung's patients' mandala-like constructions which invoke during self-meditation possible routes to imaginative health and self-direction. Like Yeats's "masks," such figures must be perpetually renewed.

After repeatedly deconstructing possible anti-selves in *Reveries* and *The Trembling of the Veil*, then after having his own intended but narrow conscious perspectives subverted by the creator's text throughout "Dramatis Personae," Yeats seems in these sections to strain to the breaking point the symbolic design of the entire work by suggesting to the reader that, as in the case of larger cultural traditions, so too in that of his own "tradition of myself," a constant "reevaluation of all values"[32] must be suffered if that tradition is to remain vital. The Anglo-Irish pose of the inheritor, which is opposed to his anti-self of the creator, the scrupulous watchmender, is itself thus threatened with opposition. The text suggests in the form of an innocent possibility that the particular pose, however labored after, is not as important as the complete absorption in the wise survivor's dream, whatever that may be. Beyond this suggestion, there is the ironic function of these sections in *The Autobiography* to be considered. With these extracts from his diary, Yeats returns—after a movement generally from childhood's comparative innocence, through the painful divisions of later experience and the apparently successful founding of his "wise" traditional viewpoint—to the original texts of his identity crisis. As such, these sections seem to call radically into question Yeats's importation into "Dramatis Personae" of his "family romance" of tradition. It also ironically plays off the traditionally Romantic spiral pattern of autobiographical development described in chapter 1 and best exemplified by Wordsworth's *Prelude*.[33] Though Yeats like Wordsworth returns to the crisis context that inaugurates his autobiographical project, he does so not with a gain in imaginative confidence, which at this point would solidify the defensive aristocratic cast of his personal myth, and so perhaps seal an unimaginative fate similar to Wordsworth's; but rather with an implicit gain in ironic distance from all his imaginative works. And yet, finally, like the significance of Oscar Wilde's "greatest short story in the world" discussed in the last chapter ("Lord, I was dead and You raised me into life, what else can I do but weep?"—*A*, 190), that of *Estrangement*

138

and *The Death of Synge* is not simply negative. As the implicit formal negation of Yeats's all-too-easy choice of a simplistic Anglo-Irish standpoint, they prepare the way, it seems clear, for a more important, truly more "positive" development. As the ironic "destruction" of the Romantic paradigm of personal growth suggests, perhaps such ironies help insure the creator's ultimate necessary detachment, his at times painful freedom from all tainted traditions or "movements"— no matter how minimal the taint or how glorious Yeats's particular blind idealization may be, for all are spawned out of that "spurious copy" of authentic culture:

> Shakespearean fish swam the sea, far from land;
> Romantic fish swam in net coming to the hand;
> What are all *those* fish that lie gasping on the
>   strand?[34]
>
> [my emphasis]

As we have seen, Yeats is always ahead of himself. Always when he writes antithetically about himself (and that is all the time), he does so, like Joyce in "The Dead" and *Portrait* especially, already distant from himself in experimental anticipation of a more fully developed, more imaginative version of the original self-interpretation that allows him to step even briefly or hestitantly ahead of himself. This anticipated later view permits him to see himself as a text of past selves, of past imaginative possibilities lived through, partially grown out of. These possibilities remain, as we have seen, still available either for his creative use or for their ironic use of him. In these extracts written long before "Dramatis Personae" it seems that Yeats is, paradoxically enough, in creative anticipation of himself again. When shortly before his death Yeats puts together *The Autobiography*, he shows how his possible aristocratic pose must necessarily be undercut by the diary extracts that follow. In their selected and re-arranged form these entries from 1909 make explicit his growing realization that the creator needs the antithetical re-evaluation of all poses if his original self-possession is to be sustained. For the increasingly more Fay-like, repeated innocent, not to recognize such irony of his tradition of himself would be criminal: "my muse is young. I am even persuaded that she is like those Angels in Swedenborg's vision, and moves perpetually 'towards the day-spring of her youth'" (A, 368).

If "Dramatis Personae"'s motto can be said to be, "It is time that I wrote my will," then that of *Estrangement* and *The Death of Synge*, for all their obvious bitter alienation from the destructive modern world, may be an even subtler, more good-humored version of "Come let us mock at the great . . . at the wise . . . at the good . . . Mock mockers after that."[35]

At half past twelve [midnight] my wife and I are alone and search the cellar for a bottle of wine, but it is empty, and so as a celebration is necessary we cook sausages. (A, 360)

Such is the Yeatsian response recorded in an impressionistic "kind of diary" (A, 358)—hence the present tense, the more colloquial style, the notation[36]—to the news that he, and not as he expected the more celebrated Thomas Mann, has been awarded the Nobel Prize for literature: a response of inexorable good cheer. Rather than simply a defensive anticipation of ironic disappointment, a cynical certainty that he will not receive the award, an ironic vision of comic fulfillment occupies Yeats's creative attention. He finds the smallest "hard" necessity an opportunity for teasing humor. This same spirit permeates even the old man's confused, often wild reveries ("But my thoughts have carried me far away"—A, 370), in which he graciously praises Sweden for its near perfect approach to his own aesthetic ideal, unity of being.[37] A kind of blithe-spirited absurdity, an intentional comic deflation of himself and a corresponding novel openness to his world, and even an ironic denigration of his own greatest achievements and highest ideals dominate the foreground in *The Bounty of Sweden*: "But such a preference [for Sweden] after so brief a visit may be capricious, having some accidental origin" (*A*, 373). Like unexpectedly winning the Nobel Prize perhaps.

Not only does Yeats dismantle the traditional Romantic image of the poet, but he disabuses us of our false reverence for all creators, and he does so intentionally. His own method of creation, imaginative self-dramatization, is no different, he claims, from the weird murmuring of "a mad old woman on the Dublin quays" also seen always talking to herself (*A*, 359). Similarly, his motive for writing is not grand passion, no urge to formal perfection, not even self-discipline any longer—only that he has not written verse for awhile. No special gift, no delicacy of feeling is his, nor is there any purpose for his still immense formal labors than that his poems might seem "all men's speech," that is, any man's (*A*, 359). As the negatives accumulate, it becomes clear that Yeats is disposing of all the accoutrements of the creator's inflated status, all his false and distorting, his spurious disguises, so that, dispossessed as any wayside tramp, he can gain a tonic distance from himself, practice, as he does throughout the section, the self-irony of the wise survivor. This self-effacement is not part of a clever formal rhetorical strategy to win our sympathy for an aging poet, with aristocratic pretensions, who writes difficult poems. The honest spirit, the chronic innocence, that marks his hilarious squabble with a proudly ignorant American winner, over whether they are objects of the Swedish royal family's smiling scorn, testifies to the comedy's authenticity. Eyes bleary, mind dazed, still partially lost in one of his many extended reveries, Yeats blithely announces to that reflexive "Jacobin," who is so sensitive about his own prerogatives: "We are the ridiculous, we are the learned at whom the little boys laugh in the streets" (*A*, 376). That Yeats, as well as his text, intends such comic reduction of self and ideals is clear from one incident in particular, in which a handsome woman at the Awards dinner asks Yeats's opinion on "the new religion of the dead" (Spiritualism) being manufactured in Paris. As Yeats launches eagerly into what seems as though it will be a long circuitous journey, full of old hopes and fears, he suddenly realizes that he has been "thinking habitual thoughts," unable, temporarily, to adapt a single word to her ear. He concludes that age may be making his mind "rigid and heavy," that, in short, he may be becoming imprisoned by his own mummy truths. His response is an almost inexplicably creative action: "I deliberately falter as though I could think of nothing more to say, that she may pass upon her smiling road" (*A*, 366). Yeats renews her innocence by ironically repeating a version of his own. He allows her to believe the symbolic text of his comic "make-believe," his personal fiction or myth of faltering, as only the oldest children can. Tragic knowledge grants Yeats this flexibility.

The central act of the comedy in *The Bounty of Sweden*, however, revolves around Yeats's own reception of his award. The prizewinner, after receiving his medal from the King and Queen, must go back up the steps to be viewed by the audience. In order not to offend royalty with his back, nor to trip and land absurdly at their feet, the recipient then must move up the steps with a crab-like "sideways movement." Before Yeats tries this—for him—difficult maneuver, he becomes captivated first by the vision of Princess Margetha's "subtle, emotional, and precise beauty" so reminiscent of Maud's and then, perhaps in defensive reaction, by the simple abstract pattern that the pieces of unnailed carpet form. To avoid looking at that fascinating—but at this point also comically dangerous—ideal beauty ("impassive with a still intensity suggesting that final consummate strength which rounds the spiral of the shell"—*A*, 364),[38] Yeats allows his attention to be focussed for him by the parallel lines that the two loosened carpet edges make at his feet. The result is that he remains facing royalty and slowly moves away from that carpet going straight up backwards without making any "sideways movement." He concludes with ironic offhandedness, capturing perfectly as he does so the sense of his all-absorbing daze: "It seems to me that I am a long time reaching the top, and as the cheering grows much louder when I get there, I must have roused the sympathy of the audience" (*A*, 365). Doubtless the crowd's gentle festival mischievousness as well: "We are the ridiculous, we are the learned at whom the little boys laugh in the streets."

It is hard to imagine the scene without breaking into a smile: the high moment of a long painful career is capped for the intentionally self-bewildering poet by a faltering, comically defensive progress—literally—to the top. Like his progress in *The Autobiography* toward imaginative innocence, Yeats is looking backward here all the way as he moves toward the conclusion. More importantly, this "impression" of the Awards ceremony is consciously repeated for us as part of, as the culmination of, the symbolic deconstruction of the creator's conventionally Romantic image. At the same time, however, Yeats exemplifies his ideal of the creator's power to transform even accident into significance. He does so here by incorporating this unforeseeable incident, like that of his intentionally faltering, into the text of that deconstruction. Chance and choice, to use the Yeatsian formula, become one, as Yeats finally realizes his anti-self in his own life. The watch-mender now shows more than his screwed-up eye to other men. He throws off all his heroic and ritual garb, abandons his sedentary position, and appears as a comically naked spectacle: the weary satyr of the antithetical quest

143

doing one last difficult turn in life's honor: "for here it is Life herself that is praised" (*A*, 367). Transcending all traditions and all meditations on the nature and necessity of tradition, but made possible only in the context of a crisis created by ever-threatened traditions is that ironic openness of repeated innocence which alone is the authentic response to the irony of time and its ceaseless absurd becoming:

All is over, and I am able to examine my medal, its charming, decorative, academic design, French in manner, a work of the 'nineties. It shows a young man listening to a Muse, who stands young and beautiful with a great lyre in her hand, and I think as I examine it, "I was good-looking once like that young man, but my unpractised verse was full of infirmity, my Muse old as it were; and now I am old and rheumatic, and nothing to look at, but my Muse is young." (*A*, 368)

Rather than face that dangerous beauty, or make that awkward movement, Yeats, like one of his own fools from the later poetry, triumphs, instead of failing, by means of his own foolishness. Analogously, by such imaginative victories over himself throughout his long career, over his own pretensions and illusions, Yeats overcomes his chronic disappointment with life and his compensating longing to surrender himself to literature, to his own all-too-tempting and all consuming artifices of eternity. He exchanges the dream-vision of perfectly humming stasis found in "Sailing to Byzantium" for the creative enactment of the tragedy's comic finale that "Lapis Lazuli" suggests. Yeats finally becomes his anti-self in *The Bounty of Sweden* and in doing so innocently anticipates himself again by ironically anticipating the "tragic joy" of the later poetry.

In *Reveries* and *The Trembling of the Veil* Yeats searches his past for traces of potential autobiographical symbols, potential images of his anti-self. By imposing a severely contrasting pattern of interpretation on the welter of such traces,

144

he provokes the sudden discovery and then almost ritual elaboration of these antithetical texts of himself. He then, in consciously repeating these texts, analytically distinguishes the pure image of his anti-self from those tainted by the influence of other people, other imaginations. His purpose is to make conscious that unconscious model of the creator which has spontaneously allowed him to survive and whose emulation would make his imagination healthier still. After exploring and apparently out-growing possible anti-selves in earlier volumes, here, in *Dramatis Personae*, Yeats has been realizing his antithetical quest by undermining any simple resolution of it. The unconscious creator in Yeats employs a dialectical irony against itself with an ever increasing and more explicitly realized conscious intention on Yeats's part. *The Bounty of Sweden* is the final and greatest example of this play of interpretation that has been discovered within ever greater portions of *Dramatis Personae*. From the minute ambiguities of the opening paragraphs' shifting temporal perspectives, through the broadly defined contrasts of Martyn and Gregory and the more elaborately "self-destructive" interpretation of Lady Gregory, Count De Basterot and George Moore, to, finally, the complete reversal, implemented by *Estrangement* and *The Death of Synge*, both of the volumes explicit Anglo-Irish viewpoint and of the Romantic pattern of autobiographical development; Yeats's text has been undercutting its own conscious positions, it has been "intentionally faltering" much as Yeats learns to do in Sweden. This is so even at the same time it offers itself—with ever less seriousness—as a climactic symbolic celebration of the Ascendancy. It is as if *The Bounty of Sweden* is one great fragment of innocence from Yeats's "tradition of myself" which ironically starts up as a result of all the antithetical interpretive play throughout *Dramatis Personae* to open him to the healthier, more comic possibilities of his own imaginative history.

145

As in certain Swedish Impressionist portraits Yeats admires, all the play of light and color, of background and foreground detail, in short, all the obvious design and the playful concern with design, in *The Bounty of Sweden* especially, is subordinated always to "the personality of the sitter" (*A*, 373), that is, to the comically realized simplifying image of the artist: "The table [aboard the Danish steamer to Sweden] is covered by an astonishing variety of cold foods, most of which we refuse because we do not recognize it, and some, such as eels in jelly, because we do" (*A*, 360).

Just as Impressionism has given new life to a tradition "sunk in convention"[39] by teaching us "to see and feel" the ordinary things again, "to take them into our hearts with the almost mystical emotion" of a strong will, to enjoy "whatever happens without forethought or pre-meditation" (*A*, 372); so, too, Yeats's text teaches him to open himself to "the shock of new material" out of which is born, as Synge believed, the only authentic style for the creator. By opening himself to the new material of his comic self-image Yeats avoids the fate of Blake and Rossetti, other "great myth-makers and mask-makers, men of aristocratic mind," who become sunk in the convention of themselves, in their own isolated geniuses, becoming at best, no more than administrators of their own great but forbidding traditions. As the "strange, mobile, disconnected" impressions of Stockholm break in on Yeats's mind, getting their "value" from its "excitement" (*A*, 358), we see *The Autobiography*'s symbolic design analogously break into the lively fragments of experience in *The Bounty of Sweden*. Yeats's effort here is not to return self-consciously, cleverly, to a hypothetical earlier style of perception. Rather it is to develop the ability to see the impressionistic life texts "innocently," without the heavy symbolic freight of portentous crises, to find a style really "flexible for expression of the emotions of *life* as they arise" (*A*, 212; my emphasis). What else can the strong inheritor of what seems to be the spurious copy of the authentic Western tradition do, but make all the best preparations he can for his having the last laugh on himself first? "He could play dirty tramp, stupid country man, legendary fool, insist on dirt and imbecility, yet play"—paradox of the text—"with indescribable personal distinction" (A, 303).

After all the award ceremonies, the grand tours, the visionary reveries, the ritual performances of the winner's most famous (not necessarily his best) work, Cathleen ni Houlihan, as well as after all the comic bounty of Sweden ("as a celebration is necessary we cook sausages"), there comes this inexplicable, unanticipated, and lightly absurd conclusion. It is the finest example of Yeats's new open style of consciousness. As Yeats's symbolic design of antitheses breaks ever closer into the present, the formerly reticent nuances of the quotidian seem to discover suddenly how to murmur with all the original self-possession that Yeats himself has learned in his life meditation:

Everyone has told us that we have not seen Stockholm at its best because we have not seen it with the trees all white and the streets deep in snow. When snow has fallen it has melted immediately, and there is central heating everywhere. While we are packing for our journey a young American poet comes to our room, and introduces himself. "I was in the South of France," he says, "and I could not get a room warm enough to work in, if I cannot get a warm room here, I will go to Lapland." (A, 377)

Unlike Dramatis Personae's opening sets of contrasting temporal perspectives these antitheses do not create the impression of a chronic disappointment with existence that, from early childhood on, only unexpected mythic visions can alleviate. Instead, Yeats's alienation, it is clear, like the snow that melts away as soon as it has fallen, has paradoxically overcome itself in time, through its comedy of distance, to allow, here in the ironic present of the text, the expression of the unaffected, wholly gratuitous naïveté of the ever playful child: "and there is central heating everywhere."

> Malachi Stilt-Jack am I . . .
> All metaphor, Malachi, stilts and all. A barnacle
>   goose
> Far up in the stretches of night; night splits and the
>   dawn breaks loose;
> I, through the terrible novelty of light, stalk on,
>   stalk on;
> Those great sea-horses bare their teeth and laugh at
>   the dawn[40]

Though time achieves its victory over the Yeats of the grand manner, albeit not without some vigorous protest, it does so attesting to the creator's final exuberant, even cheerful acceptance of his own inescapable fate in literary history: to play the fool to time's king. From the "world of old men" (*A*, 369), the only world for the few survivors of the nineties left, Yeats exits like Fay's legendary fool—"with indescribable personal distinction." He exhibits at last the only kind of style that matters, that of perpetual resilience. He seems to come, like time's own moving, most ancient image, "proud, open-eyed and laughing to the tomb."[41]

> All things fall and are built again,
> And those that build them are gay.[42]

Such gaiety is especially true of the tragic artist whose creative example of continual self-overcoming, whose ever more painfully innocent muse, makes all things of a spurious age seem by contrast in greater need of falling: "This, to repeat, would have been worthy of a great tragedian, who, like every great artist, arrives at the ultimate pinnacle of his greatness

148

only when he comes to see himself and his art beneath him—
when he knows how to *laugh* at himself."[43]

This quotation from Nietzsche expresses a perspective
on creativity that is paradigmatic of the later Yeats and for
this reason alone necessary for any comprehensive understanding of modernism's development. Though such a
stance may seem to owe much to German Romantic irony
as perfected by Friedrich Schlegel, the context here indicates
that, as in Yeats's *Autobiography*, more is involved than an
aesthetic attitude, however pervasive. Nietzsche argues that
had Wagner's *Parsifal* been a work of its author's self-overcoming, then it would have been his supreme masterpiece,
instead of what it is, his supreme mistake. Nietzsche argues
further that great artists are great not simply because they
can ironize explicitly in their own works their highest values
or even their own art, but because they do so on behalf of
life's festive celebration and man's self-overcoming, and such
celebration and self-overcoming demand sacrifices. This kind
of irony, then, is not essentially the artist's defense of his
own threatened ego, nor his clever reaction to a fragmented,
philistine world. Instead it is the long-buried creative self's
saturnalia. By their example great artists teach other men that
the possibility of becoming imaginatively in control of one's
self and one's world is still open for life's few "lucky hits."
Unlike Romantic irony, then, the exuberant liberation from
one's own works envisioned by Nietzsche here need not
entail the self-conscious appearance of the artist within his
own works to break up the reader's conventional expectations; nor does it represent a destructive increase in self-consciousness.[44] Rather such Nietzschean irony enacts an essentially creative adaptation to existence that is exemplary.
Though Paul de Man in his recent studies finds that Nietzschean irony consists simply in the constant reversibility of
his perspectives as revealed by the intricate play of his rhetorical figures, he does finally perhaps share my view that

however his irony is described it has for its end the nourishment of our imaginative ability to help ourselves to live our lives—or as I would prefer, to love our fates.[45] Such irony is unlike Kierkegaard's "unmastered irony." For it is not the expression of the dialectical imagination's fatigue. The latter appears, paradoxically enough, as the breakthrough into consciousness of mythical elements which are merely entertained for the aesthetic distraction their timeless, monumental dance affords the secretly anxious ironist.[46] Nor is it, finally, a dismal form of "self-overcoming" that involves the clever turning of irony's polar rays on oneself, with the painful results we see in Beckett's prose works, where the symbolist *auteur* deconstructs himself out of his own equally disappearing imaginative world. Rather Nietzschean self-irony, like the later Yeats's or Stevens', is "the art of terrestrial comfort"[47] for all those who insist on life's hard truths. It is an ironizing of the bitter ironist in the artist not to illustrate a religious or metaphysical belief, nor some existential truth or personal authenticity, but rather to insure the health of the human imagination, to nourish and preserve that innocence of the creator which, like the child's, can survive only if it can sublimate itself in creative play. As such, Nietzschean irony is the finest of seductions to life for the modern artist, and on our behalf: "This, to repeat, would have been worthy of a great tragedian, who, like every great artist, arrives at the ultimate pinnacle of his greatness only when he comes to see himself and his art beneath him—when he knows how to *laugh* at himself."

In *Reveries* Yeats discovers and applies—in a still rudimentary form—his autobiographical method. There he submits to imaginative scrutiny his earliest struggles to free himself from the powerful inconsistencies of a world ruled over largely by a god-like but helpless old grandfather and a self-consciously "spontaneous" father. Yeats tries to find out, apropos of his father's hypocrisies especially, whether or not the result has been simply hopeless ambivalence—and hence an ultimate imaginative decline, like his father's before him, into a pointless confusion of perspectives—or also mental resilience and so possibly creative flexibility. He in fact discovers that he possesses the unique ability, despite ever growing disappointment with the world's disorder, to make of hard necessities imaginative virtues. For example, suddenly thrown by his father into the brutal world of second-rate British boys' schools, Yeats learns how important his self-image is for his survival, learns further how to appropriate by imitation and manipulate by selective dramatization the necessary—for the time being—phases of that image. With such knowledge, he manages to exercise some control over himself and his world, enough so as not to lose completely his imaginative innocence, his openness to his own creative imagination, the major prerequisite for becoming a poet.

By imposing antithetical, almost geometrical patterns of interpretation on the memory traces of his autobiographical symbols, the later Yeats uncovers and then amplifies, symbolically repeats and elaborates, on a more self-conscious level, these earliest interpretive particulars of his heretofore largely unconscious and so undiscovered life meditation. Yeats, in pursuit of this fragmentary "buried self," contrasts heroic grandfather and confused (and confusing) father, not to compose a final synthesis for his symbolic dialectic, but to confront the original embryonic creator. This creator, different from either male figure, nevertheless is the author behind these and all the unconscious life scripts that Yeats later consciously enacts and elaborates. In the cloudy mirror of his autobiographical symbols, Yeats hopes to discover the lineaments of his self-composing anti-self. The result of that discovery is that he may then form his imaginative world according to and around such a model or "god-image." Yet it is clear, for all this, that the young Yeats at the conclusion of *Reveries* is still a fanciful aesthete, and not the consciously antithetical quester he is to become. All the world's necessary disappointments of his grand heroic fantasies and expectations force him to appear more and more like the distant spectator of his own compensatorily created formulaic imaginings. "I did not care for mere reality and believed that creation should be deliberate" (*A*, 55). All the defensive disdain of a young Stephen Dedalus resounds in such words.[48]

In *The Trembling of the Veil* Yeats seeks to transform, by means of his now perfected meditative method, the modern war of perspectives or life styles into the play of interpretations, into the dialectical moments of his dramatic autobiographical project. Such a war victimizes him and all his peers. Not how did and how must he read all the heterogeneous texts of his primal memory traces (the issue in *Reveries*), but rather how summon up, differentiate, and then emulate that antithetical creator of what must become his own coherent life text, his own life style: this is the central problem here. He re-enacts the different moments of his imaginative development from romantic hero and sage through visionary superman to *poète maudit* and the watch-mender. As a result, his (fortunately for Yeats) crisis-ridden friends become the texts—negative exempla and metaleptic figures—in his on-going and ruthless psychomachia. Like the daimon, apparently, the human creator is also attracted to tragic crisis. He needs it to inspire his play of interpretation. At the conclusion of *The Trembling of the Veil* the poet of 1917 embraces the image of the world as a hostile alien darkness that he has found in an ancient gnostic text (*A*, 257). This is an example of how great is the disappointment of the tragic ironist of his friends' fatal life crises: the would-be watch-mender, like the young poet of the 'nineties, feels his air troubled by the trembling of the veil. Like one of Eliot's famous impersonations of Dante, Yeats could say, the weight of the dreadful premonition burdening his tone: "I had not thought death had undone so many."

As he had been at the end of *The Trembling of the Veil*, Yeats is still faced in *Dramatis Personae* with a choice between seeking the consolation of a compensatory and all-embracing visionary unity (symbolized in the former volume by his vision of the Archer) and poetic composition's painful self-divisions and toils ("No mind can engender till divided into two"—*A*, 231). He now attempts therefore to set his creative priorities firmly by establishing with the help of his autobiographical method, not a simplistic either/or but rather an order of rank among his imaginative values. In pursuit of that goal, however, he must learn that his attempt to construct the ideal Anglo-Irish nucleus of a modern tradition is not the answer but is instead a species of self-victimization. It is, unless consciously embraced as a necessary and occasional fiction, the foolish vision rather than the work, of all those not impossible, that is the most fruitfully difficult. As we have seen, Yeats's own method, his own text deconstructs every blind idealization or gross condemnation. In light of this violent antithetical interaction within "Dramatis Personae," the earlier written sections of *Estrangement* and *The Death of Synge* seem like those repressed fragments of past perspectives which well up unexpectedly. As in the case of Yeats's interpretation of Edward Martyn, these irruptions from the unconscious break down habitual defenses, betray the narrowness of all purely conventional personal or cultural orders, and thereby restore to the creator in Yeats his imaginative innocence. This saving project of repeated innocence culminates in *The Bounty of Sweden*, another work written earlier than "Dramatis Personae." Here Yeats willfully becomes the comedian of the absurd by dismantling all his rigidifying disguises, all his heroic armor and priestly vestments; and, with the creator's unaccountable generosity, by according to this world of disappointment, as he did to Martyn, some of his own imaginative vitality. As Yeats inches backwards up those steps, he could well murmur to himself, behind a readier, healthier smile of self-irony, Beckett's "I can't go on, I'll go on."

In quest of the ideal paradigm for his "family romance" of tradition, Yeats is more and more exposed by his text to all the "destructive" flux of interpretation. Yet he does not become therefore merely an object worthy of the pathos of our distance. He is not finally a poor fool articulating the ego's official version of reality only to have the hidden sub-text of his "buried self's" interpretation prove at last all the more likely. Rather he seems to become the central, ever resilient player in his own work of destruction. He becomes then someone who perhaps *was* blind to the fact that he had been uncovering, even as he tried to cover them over with his ideal fancies, those more imaginative views most opposite his perversely intended ones. In other words, the foolish consciousness that the reader encounters throughout the last third of *The Autobiography* seems to learn, as it were, from the work's imaginative repetition and symbolic incorporation of both antithetical perspectives and "innocent discoveries," how to become the ironic "seer" of his own vision. As we read, the heroic poseur turns comically into the wise old *buffo* in his own comedy of distance, in his own play of temporal horizons. The fool, in short, becomes legendary, seductively and strongly protean in *Dramatis Personae*. He is at last that hero of himself who inspires our celebration of life. This is the central irony of Yeats's "tradition of myself."

The concluding speech, "The Irish Dramatic Movement," given before the Swedish Royal Academy, is the final confirmation of this view. On the one hand, it seems to say that Lady Gregory, Synge, and Yeats, by contemplating the freer, more heroic, more open world of Irish folklore and legends, originally founded the movement in the hope of creating a rich mythological literature. Such a literature, they believe, will put modern abstract Irish egos directly in touch once again with the inexhaustible archetypal depths of the race's "age-long memoried self" (*A*, 182). Instead, they have ironically left, because of the opposition of the now ruling town mentality, a somewhat lesser but still significant achievement: an increasingly realistic and authentic dialect theater. Here the old myths survive in less explicit, less heroic, and even at times in degraded "romantic" forms. The fate of their greatest "success," Synge's *Playboy*, is typical. It is a symbol of renewed and deepened disappointment: "Picturesque, poetical, fantastical, a master-piece of style and music, the supreme work of our dialect theater, his *Playboy* roused the populace to fury" (*A*, 306). In short, the Irish, not being the Greeks, are not culturally reunited by the institution of a national theater. But, on the other hand, if the speech is scrutinized more closely, especially its conclusion, it seems to create a more self-serving impression. Though not Greece, Ireland seems to have supported the growth of heroic individuals possessed of "style" and "personality." In contrast to the "splendid spectacle" of the Swedish royal family, that ideal embodiment of a living tradition, Yeats offers a spectral portrait of those great individuals who would have made, who in fact did make up, to a certain extent, the Irish "first family": "But certainly I have said enough to make you understand why, when I received from the hands of your king the great honor your academy has conferred upon me, I felt that a young man's ghost should have stood upon one side of me and at the other a living woman sinking into the infirmity of age" (*A*, 387).

Not only does Yeats perhaps seem too modest for credibility, but he also seems to be falling into the arms, almost literally, of a saving vision that will console him for the movement's disappointments. For the vision, in picturing Yeats as the last patriarch of his family romance of the Anglo-Irish

155

tradition, seeks to establish the imaginative priority, the exemplary status of his generation of inheritors and creators. It asks us to think regretfully of all that potential gone tragically to waste because of our rudely democratic age's hostility and indifference. Just as in "Under Ben Bulben" where he exhorts, as if from the grave itself, all future Irish writers to live up to his example, so, here, Yeats seeks, like Hamlet's father's ghost from the wings, to dominate the succeeding acts of literary history by his presumptuous but still compelling pronouncements. It is as if this were a Yeatsian version of the anxiety of influence in the making.

After even closer analysis, however, Yeats's speech seems, as did the rest of *Dramatis Personae*, more complex, and yet it seems neither a possible synthesis of antithetical views, nor simply an ironic cancelling of both possibilities. Rather it turns out to be another absurd repetition of innocence afforded by Yeats's "tradition of myself," by a text out of his past whose dominant perspective rises superior to the later espoused Anglo-Irish view of "Dramatis Personae." All the defensive ploys discussed above are exposed here, leaving Yeats open to the most critical and exhaustive scrutiny. Furthermore, the speech is clearly the intonation of an articulate but reverie-haunted old man who can barely take one thing at a time without dilating on each item of experience almost endlessly. Finally, it is an old warrior's last hurrah for his all but lost cause offered in the hope that it in fact may not be so:

We [the Abbey] are burdened with debt, for we have come through war and civil war and audiences grow thin when there is firing in the streets. We have, however, survived so much that I believe in our luck, and think I have a right to say my lecture ends in the middle or even, perhaps at the beginning of the story. (*A*, 387)

This is a representative sample of the wise survivor's mentality. It expresses, however hesitantly, wryly, the creator's will not to will the end. That is, it expresses the will to step back, however falteringly, from that most tempting presumption of the tradition-haunted modern man: cynically to declare the end of the idea of tradition itself so that he may then sublimely enact it.

> The swan has leaped into the desolate heaven
> That image can bring wildness, bring a rage
> To end all things, to end
> What my laborious life imagined, even
> The half-imagined, the half-written page.[49]

The ideal vision of the makeshift Irish "first family" is not the last refuge of the chronically disappointed. As presented here it is a work of the crafty watch-mender after all. Not an image to intimidate and to discourage the strong, to blight the young creators, but rather one to inspire and provoke, as well as to coerce the weak into simplistic over-reaction: an image that challenges later generations to overcome it. Succeeding players are goaded by it to take up the work, of all those not impossible, that is truly the most difficult— "sing whatever is well-made."[50] In light of this final irony, the passage on the *Playboy* is not a sign of bitterness so much as a sign of a playful, sinewy mind. There is a strange zest, a "tragic joy" if you will, taken in the inevitable reversal of all hopeful expectations. The sentence, a culminating example of Yeats's creative power to make an imaginative virtue out of disappointing necessity, seems to say with all its show of strength, in all its brash innocence, and despite the pathos of its old creator's absurd exuberance: follow my example, if you can. "My Muse is young. I am even persuaded that she is like those angels in Swedenborg's visions, and moves perpetually 'towards the day-spring of her youth'" (*A*, 365).

Hugh Kenner in "The Sacred Book of the Arts" and J. Hillis Miller in his chapter on Yeats in *The Poets of Reality* articulate two of the most influential and clearly opposing views of Yeats as a creative artist.[51] On the one hand, he seems to be for Kenner the god-like symbolist poet par excellence, who writes books, not just a series of poems, or even sequences, in which the poems are ironically related to one another through their neatly antithetical arrangement of theme, point of view, even rhetorical style. The respective volumes, at least since *Responsibilities* (1914), are of course similarly related one to another. Yeats seems to be for Miller, on the other hand, a poet of reality, who after first falling victim to his aesthetic nihilism, his defensive imperial disdain for a chaotic modern world, finds that there is more enterprise in openly walking naked amid that world's rich presences as they help constellate his now luminous consciousness. As we have seen apropos *The Autobiography* at least, neither view is completely satisfactory in itself and any suggestion that one synthesize them would seem on the face of it hopelessly naïve. Yet, as we also have seen, it is ironically out of the tradition of himself, out of those antithetically composed and arranged symbolic texts, that Yeats discovers for himself the necessity of his becoming, like his old grandfather, almost helplessly yet still heroically open to his own imaginative world. He comes finally to absorb all those ever-shifting temporal horizons. This confluence of life perspectives constitutes not primarily his new consciousness, but rather his ecstatic play of comic self-interpretations, his Romantic irony: "Some day setting out to find [self] knowledge, like some pilgrim to the Holy Land, [the artist] will become the most romantic of characters. He will play with all masks" (*A*, 318).

Of all the many theorists of interpretation Paul Ricoeur provides the best understanding of how such a development is possible. As I have indicated above, he divides contem-

158

porary hermeneutics into two major schools, that of hermeneutical suspicion and that of hermeneutical faith. The former is an analytic, reductive, generally critical method associated with the practice of Nietzsche, Freud, and Derrida. The latter is a synthetic, symbolic, generally—often dangerously—creative method associated with the practice of Hegel, Jung, and Eliade. Based on his concepts of the symbol and metaphor, Ricoeur himself recommends that we incorporate both methodologies into a more systematic and comprehensive dialectic of interpretation that would include both as different moments of one interpretive development. The symbol for Ricoeur is a double—or multiple—meaning linguistic sign which contains, thanks to the tradition of individual or collective interpretation, different semantic layers embedded with literal, imaginative, and spiritual significances. In my study of *The Autobiography* I have tried to show how Ricoeur's insights can be applied to a work of a certain genre in a particular period, so that work, genre, and world, all can be illuminated to some extent. Throughout, after first presenting Yeats's own interpretations, even risking at times the impersonation of his style, I have then attempted to expose their actual projective essences, so that their authentic status as necessary antithetical self-interpretations could then be finally revealed. The phases of Yeats's uniquely constituted imaginative growth in tragic knowledge have thus been delineated. The interpretations of Yeats's own view of Moore and of the Irish Dramatic Movement are two extreme examples of the risks of self-parody that the Ricoeurian interpreter has to take if the antithetical text is to yield all the major perspectives in its hierarchy of dialectical interpretation.

Finally, I have tried to show how Yeats's own text, in *Dramatis Personae* especially, enacts such an interpretive dialect as Ricoeur describes, and how the figure of Yeats presented by that text seems to learn from such enactment to the point where he becomes, not one of the last inheritors of a dying, narrowly defined tradition, but the most recent comic actor in the creator's ironic play of tradition. Unlike either Kenner who sees Yeats almost as Stephen Dedalus' indifferent symbolist god, or Miller who sees him finally as the more traditional, more esoteric "anticipator" of William Carlos Williams, it turns out that in *The Autobiography*, the text of his life meditation, Yeats is as much the creation as the creator of that "continuous sign-chain of ever new interpretations and adaptations" that defines his antithetical tradition of himself.[52] By imaginatively repeating and symbolically elaborating all the fragmentary texts, those memories of other people that are essentially traces of himself; and then by creating out of his extended crisis of identity a life-long autobiographical quest for a mature imagination, Yeats ironically continues to open himself to the dreaded possibility of continual self-confrontation. He must be ready to search out every feature, expose, willy-nilly, every weakness, finally love his own fate as himself:

my formula for greatness in a human being is *amor fati*: that one wants nothing to be different, not forward, not backward, not in all eternity. Not merely bear what is necessary, still less conceal it—all idealism is mendaciousness in the face of what is necessary—but love it.[53]

The work scripted by his "buried self," that scrupulous watch-mender, wills that it be so, despite the narrowest or grandest defenses of Yeats's ego. Writing his autobiography inescapably means for him that he must intend, must be willing, to re-enact yet again, like the still ecstatic dancer, every painful turn in the fiery labyrinth of life interpretation:

> I am content to live it all again
> And yet again, if it be life to pitch
> Into the frog-spawn of a blind man's ditch,

A blind man battering blind men;
Or into that most fecund ditch of all,
The folly that man does
Or must suffer, if he woos
A proud woman not kindred of his soul.

I am content to follow to its source
Every event in action or in thought;
Measure the lot; forgive myself the lot!
When such as I cast out remorse
So great a sweetness flows into the breast
We must laugh and we must sing,
We are blest by everything,
Everything we look upon is blest.[54]

Notes

Introduction

1. Wolfgang Iser, *The Act of Reading: A Theory of Aesthetic Response* (Baltimore: Johns Hopkins University Press, 1978), p. 203. Where I disagree from Iser's point of view is made clear in my review-essay of this work in *JAAC* (Fall 1979), pp. 88–91.

2. For more on this topic, see my essay-review of Ricoeur's *The Rule of Metaphor* entitled "The Irony of Being Metaphorical" in *Boundary 2* (forthcoming).

3. Harold Bloom, "The Breaking of Form," *Deconstruction and Criticism* (New York: Seabury Press, 1979), p. 5. For a critique of Bloom's influence in contemporary criticism, see my essay "The Romance of Interpretation: A 'Postmodern' Critical Style," *Boundary 2* (forthcoming).

4. The best introduction to this notion is David Hoy's *The Critical Circle: Literature and History in Contemporary Hermeneutics* (Berkeley: University of California Press, 1978).

5. The most systematic attack on the New Criticism from this perspective is that of William V. Spanos in, among other essays, "The Detective and the Boundary: Some Notes on the Postmodern Literary Imagination," *Boundary 2* (Fall 1972), 1:147–68.

6. Friedrich Nietzsche, *Ecce Homo*, Walter Kaufmann, trans. (New York: Vintage Books, 1967), p. 258.

7. W. B. Yeats, "Vacillation," *Collected Poems* (New York: Macmillan, 1967), p. 246.

8. W. B. Yeats, *The Autobiography* (New York: Collier Books, 1967), pp. 318 and 322.

1. Self-Born Mockery: The 'Play' of 'Self'-Reflection in Yeats

1. Friedrich Nietzsche, "Section 91," in Walter Kaufmann, ed. *The Will To Power*, Walter Kaufmann and R. J. Hollingdale, trans. (New York: Random House, 1967), pp. 55–56. This ironic pattern of autobiographical reflection is most fully worked out in Nietzsche's "Of the Use and Disadvantage of History for Life." The best studies of this work still remain Paul de Man's "Literary History and Literary

Modernity" in *Blindness and Insight: Essays in the Rhetoric of Contemporary Criticism* and David Couzens Hoy's commentary on Heidegger's analysis of Nietzsche's meditation on history in *Being and Time* in his "History, Historicity, and Historiography in *Being and Time*," which is collected in Michael Murphy, ed., *Heidegger and Modern Philosophy*, (New Haven: Yale University Press, 1978), pp. 329–53. Although both of these essays are extremely insightful, they do not develop as completely as Nietzsche himself does the autobiographcal dimension of such historical irony.

2. That Nietzsche in remarking on the invention of his laughing counterpart is referring to Zarathustra is highly likely given the date of this note's composition, 1885, after *Thus Spoke Zarathustra* had taken final shape. In addition, the reference to *The Birth of Tragedy* here at the time when Nietzsche was writing his new preface to that work, "Atempt at Self-Criticism," in which Zarathustra's "holy laughter," rather than Wagnerian opera represents the essence of tragedy, makes it an even stronger probability that Nietzsche's counterpart is Zarathustra.

3. See Harold Bloom, "Poetry, Revisionism, Repression," *Poetry and Repression: Revisionism from Blake to Stevens* (New Haven: Yale University Press, 1976), pp. 1–27.

4. See Roy Pascal, *Design and Truth in Autobiography* (Cambridge: Harvard University Press, 1960), p. 72.

5. The English edition, *Autobiographies*, has served as a de facto standard edition. However, the singular form of the word was Yeats's intention. I have decided to accede to Yeats's judgment in this matter, and so have used the American edition available in paperback from Colliers. This edition is the most currently accessible one. In addition, it includes Yeats's speech, "The Irish Dramatic Movement," which he gave on the reception of the Nobel Prize, an addition that increases the unity of effect produced by the last portions of the work. It is my contention that Yeats's *Autobiography* acts like a completed work, despite the periodic nature of its composition and its obvious incompleteness. In both these respects, it resembles Goethe's autobiography.

6. The words are from T. S. Eliot's "Yeats," found in Frank Kermode, ed., *Selected Prose* (New York: Harcourt, 1975), p. 256.

7. M. H. Abrams, *Natural Supernaturalism: Tradition and Revolution in Romantic Literature* (New York: Norton, 1971), pp. 13 and 77.

8. Paul de Man, *Allegories of Reading: Figural Language in Rousseau, Nietzsche, Rilke, and Proust* (New Haven: Yale University Press, 1979), pp. 173–74; 187.

9. De Man, p. 301.

10. Paul de Man, "Shelley Disfigured," *Deconstruction and Criticism: Harold Bloom, Paul de Man, Jacques Derrida, Geoffrey Hartmen, J. Hillis Miller* (New York: Seabury Press, 1979), p. 60.

11. Georg Misch, *A History of Autobiography in Antiquity*, (Cambridge: Harvard University Press, 1909 and 1954) 1:5; Jeffrey Mehlman, *A Structural Study of Autobiography: Proust, Leiris, Sartre, Lévi-Strauss* (Ithaca: Cornell University Press, 1974), p. 13.

12. James Olney, "Autobiography and the Cultural Moment: A Thematic, Historical, and Bibliographical Introduction," in *Autobiography: Essays Theoretical and Critical* (Princeton: Princeton University Press, 1980), p. 7. This volume is the most

comprehensive collection of positions on autobiography assembled to date. For equally important works, see Karl J. Weintraub, *The Value of the Individual: Self and Circumstance in Autobiography* (Chicago: University of Chicago Press, 1978) and William C. Spengemann, *The Forms of Autobiography: Episodes in the History of a Literary Genre* (New Haven: Yale University Press, 1980). Weintraub is excellent on the relationship between the development of autobiography and the emergence of the idea of the individual as the most valuable production of Western culture. But his study does not analyze closely the form of the works he treats. Spengemann does trace the development of the form from its affinities with history writing to its resemblances to poetry and fiction; but he does so in a way that avoids a direct encounter with the problematic form of autobiographical reflection as seen in Hegel. Finally, all three works do not engage in any systematic way with the challenge of deconstruction to the very idea of doing literary history as found in de Man.

13. Sprinker, *Autobiography: Essays Theoretical and Critical*, pp. 321–42. For the influence of Wilde on the formation of Harold Bloom's theory of revisionism and Edward W. Said's revisionary critical practice, especially as it appears in his *Orientalism* (New York: Pantheon Books, 1978), see my essay "The Romance of Interpretation: A 'Postmodern' Critical Style, *Boundary 2* (forthcoming).

14. See Hoy, "History, Historicity, and Historiography" in *Being and Time, Heidegger and Modern Philosophy*; and Donato, "Historical Imagination and the Idioms of Criticism," *Boundary 2* (Fall 1979), 8:39–54.

15. As quoted in Donato, pp. 45–46; and in G. W. F. Hegel, *The Phenomenology of Mind* J. B. Baillie, trans. (New York: Humanities Press, 1964), p. 752. It is from Hegel that any modern notion of reflection must stem, as pointed out in Paul Bové's "The Penitentiary of Reflection: Søren Kierkegaard and Critical Activity," *Boundary 2* (forthcoming). Yet unlike Bové, who accepts Kierkegaard's critique of Hegel completely, I must assert that it was Hegel, in his critique of the German Romantic writers and thinkers, specifically of Friedrich Schlegel and his conception of irony as "permanent parabasis," who made possible Kierkegaard's critique of reflection as a form of narcissistic self-scrutiny. I cannot engage here in an elaborate defense of the Hegelian notion of reflection as the concrete form of the speculative thinker's critique of his age and of himself, since that would take us too far afield. What I can say now is that for Hegel, as later for Nietzsche, the self discovered in the act of critical reflection is not simply the empirical ego of the alienated individual writ large across the heavens (a trick done with mirrors, of course), but rather this self is textually produced from the play of traces of earlier identifications with formative influences, such as one's educators, both living and dead. It is a more universalized, more rational, more humane and also more fragile and intermittent structuring of the mind, than that of the habitual self.

16. Hegel, p. 752.

17. Hegel, *Lectures on the History of Philosophy*, E. S. Haldane and Frances H. Simson, trans. (New York: Humanities Press, 1974), 1:444. See also Anne and Henry Paolucci, eds., *Hegel on Tragedy* (New York: Harper and Row, 1975) and Hayden White, *Metahistory: The Historical Imagination in Nineteenth-Century* (Baltimore: Johns Hopkins University Press, 1973). White's chapter on Hegel is the best introduction

to the topic of Hegel's philosophy of history, an essentially speculative view of the tragic drama of history. Two other works, these on Yeats, have been influential in the development of my understanding of Yeats's notion of tragedy: B. L. Reid's *The Lyric of Tragedy* (Norman: University of Oklahoma Press, 1961) and Thomas R. Whitaker's *Swan and Shadow: Yeats's Dialogue With History* (Chapel Hill: University of North Carolina Press, 1964). The view of Yeats's *Autobiography* that I offer here, although coming at the topic in different ways from those of Reid and Whittaker, supplements their understanding of Yeats's tragic conception of history and the individual life.

18. Yeats, "Per Amica Silentia Lunae," *Mythologies* (New York: Collier Books, 1969), p. 342.

19. See the Introduction to D. W. Robertson's *A Preface to Chaucer* (Princeton: Princeton University Press, 1961).

20. Richard Palmer's *Hermeneutics: Interpretation Theory in Schleiermacher, Dilthey, Heidegger, and Gadamer* (Evanston: Northwestern University Press, 1969) is still the best introduction to hermeneutics available in English. Palmer uses the phrase "dialectical hermeneutics" to refer to Gadamer's interpretive theory. Although the latter's position is one that can be described as in dialogue with Hegel, it is one that lacks the specificity of Ricoeur's notions of symbol and metaphor.

21. Harold Bloom, *Yeats* (New York: Oxford University Press, 1970), p. 179.

22. For a more detailed discussion of the criticism of Yeats's *Autobiography* see my essay, "The Irony of Tradition and W. B. Yeats's Autobiography," *Boundary 2* (Spring 1977), 5:679–709.

23. For a critique of Lynch's entire argument on Yeats, see my commentary in the forthcoming *JML* annual review of modernist scholarship for 1979.

24. David Lynch, *Yeats: The Poetics of the Self* (Chicago: University of Chicago Press, 1979), p. 5. *Reveries* appeared in early 1915, despite its Christmas 1914 date, and not in 1916 as Lynch has it here. Lynch's Self is not an ethical ideal that makes for community, but rather the grandiose illusion of the alienated narcissistic personality found in the theories of Hans Kohut and popularized by Christopher Lasch in *The Culture of Narcissism: American Life in An Age of Diminishing Expectations* (New York: Warner Books, 1979).

25. *The Autobiography of William Butler Yeats* (New York: Collier Books, 1963), p. 318. Hereafter all references to this work will be cited parenthetically in my text as *A* with the appropriate page numbers. Although I have compared every quotation from this edition with the English edition, *Autobiographies* (London: Macmillan, 1955), to insure by such comparison the accuracy of my citation, for reasons given above I will use the Collier *Autobiography*.

26. Joseph Ronsley, *Yeats's Autobiography: Life As Symbolic Design* (Cambridge: Harvard University Press, 1968), pp. 5 and ff.

27. Hugh Kenner, "The Sacred Book of the Arts," in John Unterrecker, ed., *Yeats: A Collection of Critical Essays* (Englewood-Cliffs, N. J.: Prentice-Hall, 1963.

28. Frank Kermode, *The Romantic Image* (New York: Vintage Books, 1957).

29. Ian Fletcher, "Rhythm and Pattern in *Autobiographies*," in Donoghue and

Mulrayne, eds., *An Honoured Guest: New Essays on W. B. Yeats* (New York: St. Martin's Press, 1966), p. 166.

30. Diana Culbertson, "Twentieth-Century Autobiography: Yeats, Sartre, Nabokov. Studies in Structure and Form," Diss. University of North Carolina at Chapel Hill, 1971, p. 99. The phrase, although Culbertson's, catches the sense of Fletcher's position, which Culbertson is reflecting on, perfectly.

31. See James Olney, "W. B. Yeats's Daimonic Memory," *Sewannee Review*, 85 (1977), the argument of which he has incorporated in "Some Versions of Memory/ Some Versions of Bios: The Ontology of Autobiography," *Autobiography: Essays Theoretical and Critical* (Princeton: Princeton University Press, 1980), pp. 259–67. Olney has elaborated on his argument that the most fruitful approach to Yeats is through an understanding of his affinities with C. G. Jung and the Platonic and Neo-Platonic philosophical tradition: see his *The Rhizome and the Flower: The Perennial Philosophy—Yeats and Jung* (Berkeley: University of California Press, 1980). Harold Bloom, of course, is the representative of the Gnostic reading of Yeats, a reading so powerful that the critic has now become more stridently Gnostic than the poet he beheld: see his *The Flight to Lucifer: A Gnostic Fantasy* (New York: Farrar, Strauss, and Giroux, 1979). Such "recollections" of ancient traditions have become a common place of cultural history, a situation Hegel saw as a necessary part of the development of the self-conscious spirit of modernity.

32. Curtis Bradford, "*Autobiographies* and 'On the Boiler,'" *Yeats at Work* (Carbondale: Southern Illinois University Press, 1965), p. 338.

33. Ibid., p. 364.

34. Yeats, *Collected Poems* (New York: Macmillan, 1967), p. 99.

35. The best treatment of this question of Yeats's Nietzschean pose and his father's negative reaction to it is found in William M. Murphy's *Prodigal Father: The Life of John Butler Yeats (1839–1922)* (Ithaca: Cornell University Press, 1978), pp. 264 and ff.

36. Yeats, *Explorations* (New York: Collier Books, 1962), pp. 152 and 144.

37. Ibid., pp. 242–43.

38. The best discussion of this topic is Søren Kierkegaard's in *The Concept of Irony* Lee Capel, trans. (Bloomington: Indiana University Press, 1971), especially pp. 132–40.

39. Bradford, p. 364.

40. The best discussion in contemporary hermeneutics of the positive effects of the distancing, universalizing effects of the mediating roles of cultural tradition is that of Paul Ricoeur in "Fatherhood: From Phantasm to Symbol," *The Conflict of Interpretations* (Evanston: Northwestern University Press, 1974), pp. 468–97. For a discussion of this essay and an application of its theoretical insights to the question of practical criticism, see my essay, "The Temptations of the Scholar: Walter Pater's Imaginary Portraits," in Leonard B. Orr, ed., *De-structing the Novel* (Troy, N.Y.: Whitson, 1980).

41. The literary archetype of the creative survivor for Yeats is Shelley's Wandering Jew. For a discussion of the importance of this figure, see chapter 3 below.

42. See C. G. Jung, "Answer to Job," in *The Portable Jung*, R. F. C. Hull trans. (New York: Viking Press, 1971), p. 630, and *Psychology and Alchemy*, R. F. C. Hull, trans. (London: Routledge and Kegan Paul, 1953), pp. 11, 12, 14, and 310. The "god-image" is that archetype of the creator which symbolizes not only the human and divine patriarchs, but, even more importantly for the individual psychology of the poet, that model of creative imagination one unconsciously enacts in one's life and work, and which, therefore, must be made conscious if one is to come to terms with oneself in an authentic way.

43. To summarize Yeats's notion briefly, one can say that the Daimon represents all those forces that press upon and shape the imagination coming from the sublime figures of the past. Like the remote author or stage-manager in an improvisional theater, the daimon hands the actor-individual a set of critical formulas that the latter must use to create his life imaginatively. I am indebted for this useful analogy to David Lynch, *Yeats: The Poetics of the Self.*

44. "Per Amica Silentia Lunae," *Mythologies*, p. 332. Another good analogy for understanding Yeats's idea of the daimon is that of Harold Bloom: viz., his notion, borrowed from Blake, of the "covering cherub." The Daimon for Yeats is as much blocking agent as mediator in our belated age: a sublime representation of the play of historical effects on the writer's psyche.

45. As de Man has shown in "Genesis and Genealogy (Nietzsche)," *Allegories of Reading*, pp. 79–102, even a text which, on the face of it, seems to be wholly determined by the genetic model of historical narration as Nietzsche's *Birth of Tragedy* seems to be is just as apparently a radically questioning text that also questions the basis of its own development. Such complexity should act as a warning to the critic who wants to elaborate a history of autobiography on the principle of a typology of progressively reflexive forms or, for that matter, on the opposite principle.

46. The briefest and most famous presentation of Yeats's brand of symbolism is "The Symbolism of Poetry," in *Essays and Introductions* (New York: Collier Books, 1961) pp. 159 and ff.

47. "Poetry and Tradition," *The Cutting of an Agate* (New York: Macmillan, 1912), pp. 128–29. "Style," "irony," "wit," and "freedom," are terms that Yeats used to interpret that surplus of meaning found in a text after all the "rules" have been satisfied, after all the conventions the writer imposes on himself have been fulfilled. The extra unique twist or play on received meaning constitutes the basis of a poet's genius. For the influence of Nietzsche on Yeats in this matter, beginning in 1902, see the chapter on Yeats in David Thatcher's *Nietzsche in England: The Growth of A Reputation, 1890–1914* (Toronto: University of Toronto Press, 1970).

48. For the former view, see Edward W. Said, "The Text, The World, The Critic," Josue V. Harari, ed., *Textual Strategies: Perspectives in Post-Structuralist Criticism* (Ithaca: Cornell University Press, 1979), pp. 161–88; for the latter position, see de Man, "Self" (*Pygmalion*), *Allegories of Reading*, pp. 160–79.

49. The basis for such a defense is, however, established in my essay, "The Irony of Being Metaphorical," *Boundary 2* (Winter 1980).

50. See Ricoeur's critique of Jacques Derrida's "White Mythology" in the former's book *The Rule of Metaphor: Multi-disciplinary Studies of the Creation of Meaning*

1. SELF-BORN MOCKERY

in Language, Robert Czerny, trans. (with Kathleen McLaughlin and John Costello, S. J.), (Toronto: University of Toronto Press, 1977), pp. 285 ff.

51. Ricoeur, *Interpretation Theory: Discourse and the Surplus of Meaning* (Fort Worth: Texas Christian University Press, 1976), pp. 94–95.

52. The best introduction to Ricoeur's career is still Don Ihde's *Hermeneutic Phenomenology: The Philosophy of Paul Ricoeur* (Evanston: Northwestern University Press, 1971).

53. Paul Ricoeur, "From Existentialism to the Philosophy of Language," Charles E. Reagan and David Stewart, ed., *The Philosophy of Paul Ricoeur: An Anthology of His Work*, (Boston: Beacon Press, 1978), p. 89.

54. See Ricoeur, "The Task of Hermeneutics," in Michael Murray, ed., *Heidegger and Modern Philosophy* (New Haven: Yale University Press, 1978).

55. "The Task of Herimeneutics," p. 92.

56. For further discussion of this topic, see my essay "The Irony of Being Metaphorical."

57. "In his *Interpretation Theory* we have Paul Ricoeur's philosophy of integral language," Ted Klein, preface to *Interpretation Theory* (p. vii).

58. Ricoeur, *Interpretation Theory*, pp. 92–93.

59. From Nietzsche's "Schopenhauer as Educator," excerpted in Geoffrey Clive, ed., *The Philosophy of Nietzsche* (New York: New American Library, 1965), pp. 329–30.

60. Yeats, "Per Amica Silentia Lunae," *Mythologies*, p. 325.

61. Ricoeur, *Interpretation Theory*, pp. 94–95.

62. Martin Heidegger, *Being and Time*, John Macquarrie and Edward Robinson, trans. (New York: Harper and Row, 1962), p. 43. The best work that I know relating Heidegger to literature and criticism on this issue of tradition is Paul Bové's *Destructive Poetics: Heidegger and Modern American Poetry* (New York: Columbia University Press, 1980).

63. I am using the term as it has been developed and adapted from its Kierkegaardian and Heideggerian origins by William V. Spanos in a series of essays during the last decade, the most important of which is "Heidegger, Kierkegaard, and the Hermeneutic Circle: Towards a Postmodern Theory of Interpretation as Dis-Closure," in *Martin Heidegger and the Question of Literature: Toward a Postmodern Literary Hermeneutics* (Bloomington: Indiana University Press, 1979), pp. 115–48. Briefly, I would characterize the notion of "repetition" I am working with here as Spanos does: as a "destructive/projective" process of reading the text that emphasizes the temporal dimension of the experience as opposed to those ways of reading that as in New Criticism and Structuralism privilege the static formal structures of the work viewed from the end intended by these structures to the virtual exclusion of the temporality of the literary work of art. I prefer, however, Paul Ricoeur's open-ended dialectical formulation of this notion in his reciprocal notion of explanation and understanding.

64. But see my essay "The Irony of Being Metaphorical," where I begin such a comparative analysis. The best study of Ricoeur and Gadamer is to be found in David Couzzens Hoy, *The Critical Circle*. Since my attempt in this work is to show

how useful Ricoeur is for the reader of Yeats's *Autobiography*, I have not gone extensively into all the affinities Ricoeur has with other thinkers.

65. See Ricoeur's discussion of Heidgger's position on this in *The Rule of Metaphor*, pp. 310 and ff.

66. Ricoeur, *The Rule of Metaphor*, p. 312.

67. *Ibid.*, p. 311.

68. *Ibid.*, p. 308.

69. In chapter 3 of *Interpretation Theory*, pp. 45–69, Ricoeur distinguishes between metaphor and symbol at some length. The gist of the distinction is that, for him, "symbol" is that figure which stands on the border between the realms of language, dreams, and the sacred as the kernel of the great narrative myths of the culture. It is, therefore, in this sense "bound" to largely unselfconscious linguistic formations. "Metaphor," on the other hand, represents the creative principle of semantic innovation in the discourse of self-reflection, in the broadest sense of that term. It is "bound," then, to changing conventions of a particular genre or form of discourse. Both "symbol" and "metaphor," however, share the feature of being a double-meaning stratified semantic structure that requires the hermeneutic art of deciphering. On the relation between Ricoeur and Yeats, see my essay, "The Irony of Being Metaphorical."

70. For Ricoeur's position on the interpreter's need to appropriate, as he is appropriated by, the text of the past, see "Explanation and Understanding," in *The Philosophy of Paul Ricoeur: An Anthology of His Work*, pp. 149–66.

71. As quoted in *The Rule of Metaphor*, p. 23.

72. Friedrich Nietzsche, *The Birth of Tragedy or: Hellenism and Pessimism* Walter Kaufmann, trans. (New York: Vintage Books, 1967), pp. 97–98. Irony, for Nietzsche, is that process of self-interpretation whereby something develops into its opposite, in accord with the "logic" of all historical becoming. The resulting self-cancellation can be seen, as Nietzsche chooses to see it, as a "self-overcomming," a "self-transcendence," in the Hegelian sense of *sich selbst aufhebend*. For a discussion of all this, see Walter Kaufmann's *Nietzsche: Philosopher, Psychologist, Anti-Christ* (Princeton: Princeton University Press, 1968), ch. 8, sec. 2. This pattern, despite all the changes in Nietzsche's style of presenting it, from the Wagnerian overtones of this early work to the exuberant playfulness of the last works, especially in *The Twilight of the Idols*, persists. Yeats, following Nietzsche's lead, understands the panache with which this pattern is enacted in one's own life as the sign of tragic insight and the only sort of freedom which, in the last analysis, man can know. For a brilliant analysis of the other forms of modern irony, see Alan Wilde, *Horizons of Assent: Modernism, Postmodernism, and the Ironic Imagination* (Baltimore: Johns Hopkins University Press, forthcoming).

73. For an excellent analysis of the way recent theorists have sought to characterize the movement of literary history, see Paul Bové, *Destructive Poetics: Heidegger and Modern American Poetry*.

74. Ricoeur, *History and Truth*, Charles A. Kelbley, ed. and trans. (Evanston: Northwestern University Press, 1965), p. 37.

75. Yeats, "Per Amica Silentia Lunae," *Mythologies*, p. 342.

170

76. Yeats, *Collected Poems*, p. 214.

77. Yeats, *Mythologies*, p. 232.

78. Harold Bloom, *Yeats* (New York: Oxford University Press, 1970), pp. 470–71.

79. Yeats, "Lapis Lazuli," *Collected Poems*, p. 292.

80. Yeats, Sec. 6 of "Vacillation," *Collected Poems*, pp. 246–47; Friedrich Nietzsche, *Thus Spoke Zarathustra*, R. J. Hollingdale, trans. (Baltimore: Penguin, 1969), p. 331. The line comes from Zarathustra's "Intoxicated Song."

2. The Prospects of Memory

1. See Marjorie Perloff, "'The Tradition of Myself': The Autobiographical Mode in Yeats," *JML* (Feb. 1975), 4:529–73. Though I agree with Perloff's contention that writing *The Autobiography* taught Yeats how to invent an effective structure for the longer lyric poem, as well as how to exploit his own self-image for dramatic purposes, I cannot agree with many of her particular readings of *The Autobiography* itself. For example, she claims that *Reveries* portrays Yeats's father as devoted to his son's education, a devotion she terms admirable. As we shall see, such is not the case in Yeats's own eyes.

2. For example, he rescued a Spanish city and never mentioned the fact. An old friend has to turn up to tell about it, and even then it is only his embarrassed silence that speaks (*A*, 2). Yeats comes to see him in terms of the figure of a King Lear (*A*, 4), who apparently suffers from Cordelia's unfortunate reticence.

3. Typically, in Yeats's view of our age, a stranger takes from an old crested cup the yellowed parchment that traces the family history and uses it to light his pipe (*A*, 11).

4. Perhaps this incident is at the origin of Yeats's later full-blown idolization of the eighteenth-century Irish Ascendancy and its lonely Victorian inheritors, many of whom go mad or drown themselves (*A*, 9, 12).

5. "Memory Harbour" was the original title of this volume of Yeats's autobiography.

6. The blue-coated man is the pilot with whom Yeats went fishing, who once held him up over the boat to see the great ships on the horizon. As he did so, the waves broke over the excited boy's head (*A*, 6).

7. "My grandfather got up in the middle of the night and acted through the mutiny [from Clark Russell's *Wreck of the Grosvenor*] as I acted my verse."

8. See Richard Ellmann, *The Identity of Yeats* (New York: Oxford University Press, 1964), pp. 216–47. Other examples are Yeats's being convinced by his vivid recollection of only a few harsh words from childhood that "all were habitually kind and considerate" (*A*, 4); and his formulation later that one should believe whatever has been traditionally believed and only reject any part of it "after much evidence" instead of following the lead of all modern philosophical movements since Descartes of doubting all first and then accepting only that which appears to be clear and

distinct, that is, indubitable, demonstratable (A, 52). That the idea of the voice of conscience originally comes to him anonymously (A, 2–3) does not affect the argument since the parent, especially the father for boys, speaks impersonally through the general forms and codes of society. This is especially true if the father, despite his and others' claims to the contrary, is a failure. That Yeats sought not to offend his father on this and other scores is clear from the many suppressed passages where Yeats speaks more openly about their relationship.

9. Yeats's earliest drama of being a hero has him leading a small band of athletic young men into a heroic but hopeless battle whose outcome is his own tragic death on the seashore. Significantly, he spends all his time preparing for that fine day by collecting many rotten and broken pieces of driftwood to build his doomed fortifications (A, 8).

10. Yeats's earliest experience of poetry is reading the stable boy's *Orange Rhymes* (A, 29). The first time he hears his father read poetry to him he is eight or nine. It happens between Rosses Point and Sligo on "a tongue of land where dead horses are buried" (A, 29).

11. It must be remembered that Yeats's method here is as much an unconscious turn of mind as it is a self-conscious aesthetic principle. The regressive dangers inherent in the method of ruthlessly seeking origins can be seen from a symbolic reading of section 18 (A, 49), which might be entitled "On the Ironic Fate of the Murderously Innocent"—to die babbling like a child: Another case can be seen in the negative example of an old white-haired poet of one of Yeats's London meditations who escapes the malicious eyes of the neighborhood by quietly going mad: living in his illusion (strictly and literally imposed on his world) that he is "under canvas on some Arabian desert" (A, 56).

12. Yeats concludes this section on his uncle by commenting at length on his own ability to change his style, and how the changed style seems to recapture some of the cold and windy light, the cold yet passionate dawn of his Sligo home, of his first world. Apparently, irony enables Yeats to relate the opposing possibilities in such a way that he can choose to realize now one, then another, without becoming one-sided or merely aesthetic in the process.

13. For example, do poetry and sculpture exist to keep our passions alive, or do the arts only make us more sensitive and so increase our unhappiness? The young Yeats grandly vows to give up his poetic career if he cannot be certain that the arts make us happier (A, 57).

14. Yeats originally projects an imaginary past of lost loves for that dark romantic face only to learn that a more bitter past lies behind its carefully preserved features. Dowden gave up a promising poetic career for the security of the academy, "wisely" writing purely conventional poetry thereafter, when writing at all.

15. Another source for Yeats's own method is beginning to be elaborated here.

16. See Paul Ricoeur, "What is a Text?" in David Ramussen's *Mythic-Symbolic Language and Philosophical Anthropology: A Constructive Interpretation of the Thought of Paul Ricoeur* (The Hague: Martinus Nijhoff, 1971); and "Metaphor and the Main Problem of Hermeneutics," *NLH* (Autumn 1974), pp. 95–110.

17. Before coming under Chatterjee's brief influence, Yeats would hide from

his old schoolmaster in another of Dowden's rooms rather than face him. After that momentous meeting, Yeats can confront the man on the street for the latter's disparagement of his and his friends' esoteric beliefs (A, 57, 59). Yet, typically, Yeats attributes this last grandiloquent gesture to his too great alarm at running into him in that way (A), 59).

18. Yeats confesses that he did not discover this truth until later: "I did not discover that Hamlet had his self-possession from no schooling, but from indifference and passion-conquering sweetness, and that less heroic minds can but hope it from old age" (A, 62).

19. O'Leary, for example, lent him the poem of Davis and the Young Ireland of whom he had known nothing, and O'Leary did not, "although the poems of Davis had made him a patriot, claim that they were very good poetry" (A, 63).

20. Yeats easily tricks Taylor by asserting that five out of six people have seen a ghost, of course, preparing these in the room beforehand. So Taylor falls right into Yeats's net. And though he rarely heard Taylor read poetry, it is often his voice Yeats still hears when he remembers his father reading to him (A, 65, 66).

21. Yeats says that from O'Leary, either directly or indirectly, "has come all I have set my hand to since" (A, 67).

22. Similarly, a strange vision at Ballisodare that brought him back to the superstitions of his childhood results finally in sleepless doubt. "I kept asking myself if I could be deceived . . . I hurried on doubting, and yet hardly doubting . . . I was always ready to deny or turn into a joke [especially with his argumentative father] what was for all that my secret fanaticism. When I had read Darwin and Huxley and believed as they did, I had wanted, because an established authority was upon my side, to argue with everybody" (A, 51–2).

23. From the first visions (A, 6) through that at Ballisodare to this seance, we increasingly sense that for Yeats at times only a major influx of the supernatural would make life worth living, and yet, even that, we are finally assured by the pattern of his development, ultimately would serve to make this life by contrast all the more unbearably bleak and tragic.

24. Diana Culbertson, in "Twentieth Century Autobiography: Yeats, Sartre, Nabokov. Studies in Structure and Form," Diss. University of North Carolina at Chapel Hill, explains this incident by relating it to three other similar ones (A, 190, 206, 319), with the result that the graveside quarrel from Deirdre becomes the archetype for our age: "'And isn't a poor thing we should miss the safety of the grave, and we trampling its edge'" (A, 313).

25. Joseph Ronsley's interpretation, from Yeats's Autobiography: Life As Symbolic Pattern (Cambridge, Mass.: Harvard University Press, 1968), p. 146, n. 48, is the strangest of them all, finding in a crabbed and confused passage from On the Boiler (Dublin: Cuala Press, 1939, p. 22) the explanation for the final lines of this conclusion. Ronsley, who makes much of Yeats's symbolic drama in his reading of The Trembling of the Veil, nevertheless repeatedly seeks the meaning of the autobiography outside the text in Yeats's other, more esoteric works, such as A Vision. The result is a programmatic reading that oversimplifies the complexities or even ignores the most obvious particulars. For example, he sees only the thematic cluster of nation,

literary tradition, and supernatural belief in the opening passages of *Reveries*. That is, he reads that particular configuration from the autobiographical sketch, "If I Were Four and Twenty," back into this opening in a very schematic fashion. He sees so little of the fragmentation at first that he calls this opening section Edenic. He needs to see, for the fulfillment of his scheme, Yeats begin in complete innocence, then fall into experience, so that he can then rise triumphantly into manhood.

26. This remark in its context primarily refers, of course, to Yeats's efforts to become a painter, to follow in his father's footsteps. However, I think it is also an appropriate comment on his life-long aesthetic project and on one major obstacle that continues threatening to block its realization: his father's intimidating influence and his own compensatory defensive aesthetic attitude.

3. The Genius of Technique

1. Majorie Perloff in her article for *JML* (Feb. 1975), 4, 529–73, "'The Tradition of Myself': The autobiographical Mode in Yeats," argues that, in essence, Yeats is deluding himself and us here when he says that he came to see into that mind. The significance of Yeats's reflection is not its unknowable relation to whatever the truth of the matter might be; it is the way he uses the figure of Maud Gonne to make a self-reflecting comment on the entire course of a life in our age. Yeats in the preface to this section of *The Autobiography* claims "an historian's right" over the experiments that he says were his friends' lives, and he records and analyzes them in fact as a historian of his own self must: "I have not felt my freedom abated. . . . I have kept back nothing necessary to understanding" (*A*, 74). See also *Collected Poems*, pp. 90, 212, for important portraits of Maud Gonne.

2. The apparently opposing ideas of interpretive discovery and invention are not finally incompatible if we remember that all the unsettling oppositions that define our world are already projected and realized there by the system of human language and culture and that Yeats then is only discovering and perfecting old inventions for the purpose of dramatically ordering his imagination: "Now we read disharmonies and problems into things because we think only in the form of language. . . ." Friedrich Nietzsche, in Walter Kaufmann, ed., *The Will to Power*, Walter Kaufmann and R. J. Hollingdale, trans. (New York: Random House, 1967), p. 283, n. 522.

3. Though the concept of play, in the questionable form of "free-play," has suffered a current revival in the work of Jacques Derrida, the meaning of the term for me is primarily that of the idea of a play of forces. This idea can cover a wide spectrum of related ideas, such as that of drama, child's play, adult's games, even that idea contained in the expression "there's too much play in the lines." The play of interpretation in *The Trembling of the Veil* means essentially the drama of Yeats's interpretive response to a crisis of identity in which he seeks to transform the conflicts of that crisis into the aesthetic play of antithetical composition. As we shall see, the result of this play is not Derrida's joyous, supposedly Nietzschean affir-

mation of a finally centerless world structure; rather it is a necessary painful formalization of the conflicts which in its near perfect expression of them does little to alleviate the pain. Instead it only tends to increase the poet's sufferings. It becomes like the formal, intellectualized defense of the neurotic: obviously inescapable especially for the subject-host.

4. Here, as throughout, the dramatic metaphor structures Yeats's central interpretive commentary. The image that Yeats comes up with to describe the effects of Florence Farr's crisis on her mind derives from his memory of a children's game called Spilikens, the object of which is to pick out like pieces of bone from the pile with a hook, if you can (A, 81). Notice that the use of a child's game does nothing to alleviate the painful spectacle of her crisis, but if anything ironically increases it. The crisis that Wilde goes through is of course famous. That of Henley is the failure of his search and the pathetic loss of his beloved young daughter (A, 198–99). That of Morris is his being faced with the dessication of the language. Only by writing slowly and learnedly could he hope to overcome that situation. Or so Yeats projects. Since Morris lacks a self-conscious awareness of his own antithetical nature, he cannot fuel his poetic efforts adequately enough to suit Yeats in the final analysis. Instead, he has to imagine new conditions of making for the craft-arts (A, 95–96).

5. See especially, "Per Amica Silentia Lunae" (1917), Mythologies (New York: Collier Books, 1969), pp. 352–53. In this respect they resemble those spontaneously generated autonomous images or archetypes that enter our conscious minds completely formed, without our calculation, from the collective unconscious. Their numinous power, C. G. Jung argues, makes us experience them as if they were subjects, living beings within us, and not simply the objects of our internal perceptions. See "Answer to Job," The Portable Jung (New York: Viking Press, 1971), p. 525.

6. See Per Amica, p. 344, where Yeats quotes with approval a letter of Goethe's on the subject of the living symbol: "You have discovered how, if you can but suspend will and intellect, to bring up from the subconscious anything you already possess a fragment of." Yeats suspends will and intellect by using the crisis of interpretation to exhause judgment repeatedly. See also, Per Amica, p. 347. Yeats describes the moment of vision in this passage as leaving "some trace, a sudden silence as it were, in the midst of thought—perhaps at moments of crisis a faint voice." The term trace, however, also has a current critical notoriety in the work of Derrida. There it is used to suggest that written and not spoken language has priority in the formation and determination of the human mind. Furthermore, the term is also used to suggest that it is inappropriate to talk about perception, for we never experience a world outside our own "textual" articulation and our reading of these "traces." Though I see the relation between this usage of the word "trace" and my own, I intentionally do not choose to draw any closer parallels, nor to mark bodily the differences, because the question of whether or not the mind finally escapes, even for a brief moment, the prisonhouse of language is still a metaphysical question that perhaps can never be settled to any one's satisfaction, but instead only keeps the "game" of metaphysics and its announced deconstructions going.

7. The "buried self"—a term appropriated by Yeats from Matthew Arnold— is a dual entity. One part consists of the anti-self, which might be considered anal-

ogous to the Jungian Shadow in some respects and to the Persona in others, but which primarily is analogous to what Jung calls "the god-image" or divine archetype. The other part of the "buried self" consists of the Anima Mundi, which is clearly identical to the Jungian Collective Unconscious, though Yeats finds his systematic support for this notion in the speculations of Henry Moore, a seventeenth-century "esoteric" philosopher. The Anima Mundi is the world that the "god-image" is primarily related to. When I use the term "buried self" I mean to refer only to the anti-self or god-image. When I mean to refer to the Anima Mundi I use that term or a closely related one such as the Great Mind or the Great Memory, both of which Yeats himself uses.

8. Yeats, *Collected Poems* (New York: Macmillan, 1966), p. 159. Though this passage is not cited by Yeats in *The Autobiography*, as are other poems, a good deal of the rest of "Ego Dominus Tuus" is (*A*, 184). See also *Per Amica*, p. 337: "We meet always in the deep of the mind, whatever our work, wherever our reveries carry us, that other will." The idea of this "other will" brings up Yeats's belief in the Daimon, the now coherent spirit from another age that, being most opposite the disorderly living man, creates all our creative and destructive conflicts. Belief in the spirit is not necessary for the reader of Yeats. A belief in the power of language, however, to appear like a daimon, an invading other, might be. Yeats's systematic vocabulary often proves difficult. For example, his term "antithetical," means primarily an extreme opposition, which seems incapable of being resolved, such as that existing between the created text and the chaotic man. In conjunction with my use of the term "dialectic," defined in chapter 1, some confusion might arise. "Dialectic" is the difficult process of allowing extreme, apparently irreconcilable antitheses to yield an unexpected momentary synthesis. The sudden irruption of one of those mediating autobiographical symbols into the conscious mind from the unconscious is an example. The process of creating a written text "temporalizes" Yeats's antithetical imagination into a symbolic dialectic that is open-ended. What I mean by other terms such as "symbol," "vision," "imagination," or "creation" should be specified now, too. "Symbol" is a double—or—multiple-meaning linguistic entity which arises from the unconscious into the conscious mind under the pressures of becoming a formal element in the composition of a written text. It incorporates within its dialectically-related semantic layers archetypal as well as particular meanings that not only point back to the author's past but also forward to the formation of the final text. "Vision" means the manifestation or discovery of a symbol by consciousness. "Imagination" or "creation" means the entire process of Yeats's meditative method, which in its inclusion of both painful discovery or antithetical analysis, and symbolic composition or visionary synthesis is at least distantly related to Coleridge's famous description of the secondary imagination in chapter 14 of *Biographia Literaria*.

9. Yeats regrets that this event was not made common knowledge until after Parnell's death, after the absence of a heroic center for Ireland finally becomes a reality: "What excitement there would have been, what sense of mystery would have stirred all our hearts . . ." (*A*, 156). Hardly a mature attitude, but certainly an aesthetic one.

176

3. THE GENIUS OF TECHNIQUE

10. The image comes from Yeats's memories of Sir Charles Gavan Duffy, the insensitive literary patriarch of the failed nationalist literary movement of the 1840s and '50s, "Young Ireland." Or so Yeats sees him. The fire motif, along with the motifs of the shell and of wax, are clearly obvious ways of structuring the commentary in *The Trembling of the Veil*.

11. Opposed to Parnell's example are those of Lionel Johnson and John O'Leary. Johnson's austerity of face and form, so symbolic for Yeats of the almost Grecian nobility and classical taste of his learned friend's best verse (*A*, 148), and O'Leary's heroic integrity, his speaking the truth for self-expression's sake and not for fear or favor of others ("My religion is the old Persian, to pulll the bow and tell the truth"—*A*, 141) save Yeats from his helpless immolation in the bitter partisan rivalries and abysmal lack of taste that afflict his groups. The immediate result of their example is to persuade Yeats to continue in his vain hope that the Irish situation, apparently ripe like soft wax for the seal, can really receive and retain the heroic imprint (*A*, 140). As in *Reveries* (*A*, 138), the image of wax symbolizes the political situation in Ireland (*A*, 138, 142). See also "Nineteen Nineteen."

12. See Yeats's comment on his treatment of Dowden in a letter to his father (*Letters*, p. 606): "he was helpful and friendly when I began to write and I give him credit for it. But in my account of Dublin I had to picture him as a little unreal, set up for contrast beside the real image of O'Leary." To fulfill his formal design of symbolic psychomachia, Yeats has to project onto Dowdon his own youthful unreality so as to make it contrast sharply with O'Leary's idealized heroic vitality in a way that would leave Yeats free to appropriate its "real image" without spoiling the unity of his work.

13. This aspect of Yeats's treatment is clearer in Russell's case. But even with Parnell, Yeats fits him into his own symbolic framework; he has him fitted to be hung like the other portraits.

14. As Yeats suggests in the preface (*A*, 74) and states explicitly in the "The Tragic Generation" (*A*, 210), "'our air is disturbed,' Mallarmé said, by 'the trembling of the veil of the temple,' or 'that our whole age is seeking to bring forth a sacred book'" to replace the now discredited Book. "Some of us thought that book near towards the end of the last century, but the tide sank again." This longing explains why "the greatest poet to write English in our time" would sit in Edward Martyn's neo-Gothic hall and ask for all the lights but one little Roman lamp to be extinguished so that amid the great vague shadows and faint light that would conceal or mask a meaningless world and its decadent ornament he might picture himself the hero of some incredible Romance. As part, in short, of that new sacred, saving text, whose organic design of a quest for self would satisfy imaginative desire and screen a sensitive nature. In this situation the shadows are free to take the form of those "imaginary people," easily re-imagined and re-interpreted by Yeats, from the great visionary texts of the past. They now can begin to utter their mythological truths to a desperate and confused man. Real people are harder to re-imagine with any satisfactory consistency.

15. Here Yeats is like some latter-day Hamlet figure defensively irrational—in some parts at least—about his class affinities and aspirations.

16. It is significant that so much depends upon this "crazy" experiment and that it enters the site of the text here. Yeats needs to believe its results that badly. By "site of the text" I mean that special region or zone of attention in Yeats's imaginative vision before the blank or half-filled page that is like one of those shut-in mysterious places of his childhood (*A*, 11) or shadowy places where the mind plays seriously in what Jung terms a *temenos* spot and waits for something marvelous to happen; in Yeats's case, for the written text finally to be composed.

17. See the above quoted passage (the epigraph) in which Yeats compares the "work" of artists to that of alchemists. See also Peter Alt and Russell K. Alspach, eds., *The Variorum Edition of the Poems of W. B. Yeats* (New York: Macmillan, 1973), p. 778 for the often cited, untitled poem: "The friends that have I do wrong/When ever I remake a song/Should know what issue is at stake:/It is myself that I remake."

18. See *Per Amica*: "All happy art seems to me . . . a hollow image of fulfilled desire, but when its lineaments express also the poverty or the exasperations that set its maker to work, we call it tragic art" (p. 329).

19. See Thomas Whitaker, *Swan and Shadow* (Chapel Hill: University of North Carolina Press, 1964); see also *Per Amica* (p. 336): "When I think of life as a struggle with the Daimon who would ever set us to the hardest work among those not impossible, I understand why there is a deep enmity between a man and his destiny, and why a man loves nothing but his destiny."

20. See *Per Amica*, p. 325: "But when I shut my door and light the candle I [at first] invite a marmorean Muse, an art where no thought or emotion has come to mind because another man has thought or felt something different, for not there must be no reaction, action only . . . but for a moment I believe I have found myself and not my anti-self. It is only the shrinking from toil, perhaps, that convinces me that I have been no more myself than is the cat the medicinal grass it is eating in the garden."

21. Aubrey Beardsley (*A*, 221–23) is one of Yeats's major examples of the artist as victim to his own genius, the Yeatsian version of the *poète maudit* or suffering poet. Frank Kermode, in *The Romantic Image* (New York: Vintage, 1957), has investigated this tradition of interpreting the poet in relation to Yeats. The poet, ignored or persecuted actively by an insensitive and hostile world, must suffer the even greater burden of his self-torturing dream visions of an ideal perfection that is impossible to realize in our world, even within the beautiful forms of art. At best art can only suggest the faint outlines of those visions to tantalize us all. As can be seen, Yeats adapts this tradition to his own idea of the creator's quest for his anti-self in *The Autobiography*.

22. This is just another way in which Yeats uses the dramatic metaphor to structure his interpretation in *The Trembling of the Veil*. Typically, these plays reflect for Yeats a movement from a pathetic realism with pretensions to tragedy to the bitter, mechanical comedy of the absurd. Also typically yeats's reactions are divided. In the case of both plays, while at the performance, Yeats takes the side of the plays, supporting their energy if nothing else, fearful of being thought on the side of the washerwomen in the audience who oppose the plays. But later, in conversation

178

with close friends, or in private contemplation, he thinks better of his earlier responses. It is in his conversation after seeing "Ubi Roi" that Yeats utters his famous remarks about the Savage God. He also gives a schematic history of the growing fragmentation and decline in the process: "After Stephane Mallarmé, after Paul Verlaine, after Gustave Moreau, after Puvis Chavannes, after our own verse, after all our subtle colour and nervous rhythm, after the faint tints of Conder, what more is possible? After us the Savage God." As might be expected, Yeats's history is the development of the arts as symbolized by the figures of the creators.

23. See *Per Amica*, p. 337.

24. The modern strategy of a radical deconstructive irony achieves its finest and fullest expression in Nietzsche: "Parmenides said, 'one cannot think of what is not':—we are at the other extreme, and say, 'what can be thought of must certainly be a fiction'" (*The Will to Power*, p. 291, n. 539).

25. E. M. Forster, *Aspects of the Novel* (New York: Harcourt, Brace, and World, 1927), pp. 149–71; Harold Bloom, *A Map of Misreading* (New York: Oxford University Press, 1975). According to Bloom metalepsis is a "troping upon a forerunner's tropes," that is, using one distinctive kind of rhetorical figure of a poetic father in order to allude to his entire imaginative stance, so as to re-interpret, to misread him creatively. While one might argue with Bloom's conclusions, his concise definition of metalepsis seems accurate enough for my purposes. Compare J. Hillis Miller, "Deconstructing the Deconstructors," *Diacritics* (Summer 1975), 5:24–31. I would argue that metalepsis, then, is a form of synecdoche, that Yeats uses his particular images of his friends to allude to their whole life styles with the ironic result, however, that as they are re-interpreted, "misread" according to his symbolic design, the difference between (once) living human beings and formal elements in a text becomes increasingly apparent, increasing thereby the tension of Yeats's autobiographical play, as his dramatic meditative method requires.

26. The concept of repetition as an "existential category" is developed fully and in all its subtlety by Kierkegaard in *Repetition*, Walter Lowrie, trans. (New York: Harper and Row, 1964). Its most succint definition comes in contrast to the traditional philosophical category of recollection (p. 52): "When the Greeks said that all knowledge is recollection they affirmed that all that is has been; when one says that life is a repetition one affirms that existence which has been now becomes." All that a man has unconsciously been, he now wills consciously to become by projecting the discovered patterns of his existence into the emerging future, so that he might become thereby truly authentic—no matter how obnoxious or distasteful or sad his authenticity may turn out to be for others. Developing Kierkegaard's ideas of autobiography, which would seem to be exclusively defined by recollection, this means that all that Yeats has read unconsciously into his life now finally becomes a conscious symbolic interpretation of that life. He then not simply projects his symbolic design into the future, but anticipates its shape as it emerges at the site of the text in the form of his found and then chosen simplifying image. Repetition, then, is the "temporalization" of recollection in terms of an individual's unique life text.

27. The Dead in Yeats's speculations (*A*, 251; *Per Amica*, p. 356–58) actually re-

179

live their past lives backwards toward the source, as it were, till they possess in one single moment a vision of all of themselves. The Dead, of course, can have this privilege; the artist can only know that he at times vainly yearns for it.

28. In the larger context of the entire section, Yeats is comparing himself and Synge, both implicitly—as usual—and explicitly. Yeats recalls, for example, his impression of Synge's early verse and prose: like a breath-befogged windowpane (*A*, 230). Another clear case of projection.

29. See "Answer to Job," *The Portable Jung*, pp. 524 ff.

30. The clearest expression of this "ideal" in Yeats's poetry is enacted in "Lapis Lazuli": "Gaiety transfiguring all that dread./All men have aimed and found and lost:/Black out; Heaven blazing into the head:/Tragedy wrought to its uttermost."

31. See Frank Kermode, *The Romantic Image*.

32. William v. Spanos, "The Detective and the Boundary: Some Notes on the Postmodern Literary Imagination," *Boundary 2* (Fall 1972), 1:147–68, see especially p. 158; *The Variorum Edition of the Poems of W. B. Yeats*, p. 845.

33. Yeats's self-conscious awareness of an audience for his art keeps it from becoming hermetic like Mallarmé's and so keeps it a drama between his desire and need for such a pure art and his need to express to others the reasons why he has such conflicting desires and needs. The bitter need to explain himself at least to one, indifferent other paradoxically impels his symbolic art of self-interpretation and ironic disappointment. See "Words," *CP*, pp. 88–89: "That every year I have cried At length/My darling understands it all,/Because I have come into my strength,/ And words obey my call; That had she done so we can say/What would have shaken from the sieve?/I might have thrown poor words away/And been content to live."

34. Apparently "the old trouble" is that dread and need of masturbation he talks more openly about in *Memoirs*, Denis Donoghue, ed. (New York: Macmillan, 1971). Significantly, he equates that "old trouble" with his early lush, Romantic style that Joyce labelled insightfully as onanistic.

35. See *Memoirs* (New York: Macmillan, 1971), pp. 88 and ff.

36. See *Per Amica*, p. 337: "The poet finds and makes his mask in disappointment . . ."

37. Two of Yeats's justifications: since science has won, through much ridicule and persecution, the right to "explore whatever passes before its corporeal eye," should not literature demand the same right "for all that passes before the mind's eye and merely because it passes" (*A*, 217–18). Note the echo of Pater. And, since historical Christianity and its culture "has dwindled to a box of toys," might it not be amusing "to empty the whole box on to the counterpane" (*A*, 223). He imagines that Beardsley's last-minute conversion is a form of the latter kind of amusement.

38. The image occurs at the conclusion of "The Tragic Generation" as one of those fragmentary impressions with which he concludes three of the five books of *The Trembling of the Veil* as if in mockery of the world's fragmentation.

39. Two of the related visions recorded here are important. In one he hears a voice say "the love of God is infinite for every human soul because every human soul is unique, no other can satisfy the same need in God" (*A*, 252). This is one example of Yeats's longing to escape the painful complexities of experience. The

other vision is one in which a voice speaks through his own stricken lips, also at dawn: "We make an image of him who sleeps and it is not him who sleeps, and we call it Emmanuel" (*A*, 252). This is Yeats's defense against those painful complexities, the Mask, an idea found in despair of ever realizing the ideal of divine unity described above. Finally, Yeats accidently discovers, years later as he is writing this portion of *The Autobiography* (*A*, 253), a Gnostic Hymn included in Burkitt's *Early Eastern Christianity*. The Hymn tells of "a certain King's son who being exiled, slept in Egypt—a symbol of the natural state—and how an angel while he slept brought him a royal mantle, and at the bottom of the page I found a footnote saying that the word mantle did not represent the meaning properly for that which the Angel gave had the exile's own form and likeness." At last Yeats finds traditional support for a cherished antithetical "conviction" (*A*, 253).

40. For another example of poems which appear in *The Autobiography* as if arising out of Yeats's story of his life and fragmentary times, see p. 130 for "The Second Coming."

41. *Per Amica*, p. 342.

42. *Ibid.*, p. 332.

4. The Faltering Image

1. Throughout this chapter I use *Dramatis Personae* to refer to the entire last third of *The Autobiography*, and "Dramatis Personae" to refer to the opening section alone.

2. Yeats, *Collected Poems*, p. 229.

3. This "tradition" includes all Yeats's poetry, critical prose, and plays, as well as his autobiographical texts.

4. This term, originally Freud's, has been recently adopted—and adapted—by Harold Bloom in his *The Anxiety of Influence* and *A Map of Misreading*. Though Yeats is certainly open to either a Freudian reading, or a Bloomian "mis-reading," he is sufficiently self-aware concerning these matters at least to be "there," as it were, before his critics, as illustrated by his construction of his own ideal imaginative relationship among the Anglo-Irish inheritors. I intend by my use of the term to critically call into play all these resonances for the purpose of showing how Yeats is led by his tradition of himself to deconstruct his own defensive self-serving imposition of a narrowly defined paradigm of tradition. By deconstruction I mean the creative dismantling or "undoing" of a particular interpretive edifice implemented by the more open, threatening imaginative possibilities that arise in the unconscious context of the ironic Yeatsian text.

5. Yeats sees Martyn and Moore as figures out of old folktales, that is, as comic figures of the saint who needs, even as he despises, his devil in order to define himself, and vice versa.

6. Martin Heidegger in *Being and Time*, John Macquarrie and Edward Robinson, trans. (New York: Harper and Row, 1962), pp. 41–61 and 182–209, is responsible

for introducing, in this form at least, the notion of "destruction." Briefly, he means by the term the critical analysis of a philosophical text, like Kant's *Critique of Pure Reason*, the destructive interpretation of such a text, for the purpose of uncovering the covered over significance that the text, if not its author, intended to uncover for itself but did not because of the author's own narrowness or imprisonment within then reigning conventions of thought and language. I use the term throughout in a related, but somewhat different way. Here it is Yeats's own text that carries out the largest burden of the "destruction" that Heidegger leaves to the interpreter. In other words, it is a matter of degree and emphasis. It is because neither Heidegger nor any of his disciples are open to the dreadful reality of the unconscious or subconscious, either in the accepted psychoanalytic sense or in the archetypal sense Yeats himself accepts, that they must lay all of the burden of destruction on the interpreter's shoulders. The result is that they are then exposed to the unanswerable charge of critical relativism. That every one's interpretation is one's own is a truism; but that this then must imply the absence of any authoritative contact between the consciousness enacted in the text and the interpretor's own is just as truly a specimen of critical nihilism. I prefer Nietzsche's formulation of the situation: that just as each creative "giant" calls across "the desolate intervals of time" to his fellows, so they all sometimes deign to signal to critical "dwarfs" who make up "the republic of scholars." See *Philosophy in the Tragic Age of the Greeks* Marianne Cown, trans. (Chicago: Henry Regnery, 1962), p. 32.

7. The idea of "make-believe," "fictions," "myth" consciously adopted, what Ellman calls "affirmative capability" (*The Identity of Yeats*, pp. 216 ff.), are all notions associated with a certain stance of modern poets. Perhaps still the most comprehensive description of such a stance is Hans Vaihinger's *Die Philosophie des Als Ob* (1911). However, the most succinct and probably most influential version of the idea of "fiction," outside of Wallace Stevens' "supreme fiction" and Conrad's "true lie," can be found in Nietzsche. See, for one "cheerful" example, *Beyond Good and Evil*, Walter Kaufmann, trans. and ed. (New York: Vintage, 1966), p. 35. But Nietzsche's most serious discussion of this idea occurs at the conclusion of *On the Genealogy of Morals*, R. J. Hollingdale and Walter Kaufmann, trans. (New York: Vintage, 1967), pp. 160 ff. Here Nietzsche not only reiterates his contention that to live means to create an essentially fictional world and then to impose it on the flux of becoming, but also entertains the "dangerous" question of "what is the meaning of all will to truth" (p. 160), which wants to expose, for purposes of cynical, nihilistic denigration, all man's necessary fictions. Though Nietzsche himself exposed many of those fictions, that of inherent rational or moral orders in the world, that of a stable ego, that of impersonal objective viewpoints, etc., he did so to overcome just such nihilism which depends on the fiction of abstract objectivity in particular to reduce all differences between stronger and weaker individuals so that all may be equally mean and powerless abstract counters as the nihilistic ego feels itself to be. These issues are all too complex to settle here. Suffice it to say that both Nietzsche and Yeats celebrated the artist's extraordinary capacity for "make-believe" as almost a sacred power, as the *only* sacred power.

8. See D. C. Muecke's two books, *The Compass of Irony* (London: Methuen,

1969) and *Irony* (London: Methuen, 1970), for the best studies on the subject. Only Alan Wilde in his study published in *boundary 2*, "Barthelme Unfair to Kiergaard: Some Thoughts on Modern and Post Modern Irony," *boundary 2* (Fall 1976), 5:45–70, has effectively exposed the attitude behind such temporal irony as described here in relation to Yeats. Wilde succinctly indicates its essence by terming it an "irony of assent."

9. Yeats comes to believe that all social conventions, cultural phenomena, even a culture's concepts are "fictions," determined by our language and the structure of belief built into that language. That he does so after immersing himself in Nietzsche is not surprising: "The Incarnation invoked modern science and modern efficiency, and individualized emotion. It produced a solidification of all those things that grow from individual will. The historical truth of the Incarnation is indifferent, though the belief in that truth was essential to the power of invocation. All civilisation is held together by the suggestions of an invisible hypnotist—by artificially created illusions. The knowledge of reality is always in some measure a secret knowledge. It is a kind of death" (*A*, 326).

10. Yeats always listens to her proverbs: "You should give up journalism. . . . The only wrong act that matters is not doing one's best work" (*A*, 273).

11. Lady Gregory, for example, disapproving of Yeats's plan to open *The Countess Cathleen* first in London, prevails finally upon him by her power to persuade him to act upon the moment (*A*, 266).

12. Though Yeats quotes the phrase of an anonymous folk saying, here he appropriates it for his own.

13. It is almost as if Moore, and not Stanislaus Joyce, were the prototext for Shawn to the Archetypal creator's Shem. Moreover, Yeats originally thinks of his rival as an ally in the battle against England's exported vulgar materialism (*A*, 229). With the publication of *Esther Waters*, Yeats's hope suddenly wanes. So Yeats turns as suddenly against that hope's betrayer.

14. They work together for a number of years. *Diarmuid and Grania* is the one play they jointly sire.

15. Martyn becomes a financial backer of the Abbey and even a contributing playwright (with Moore's help). Only his strong and unfortunate confidence in the theological judgment of the higher clergy at the time of *The Countess Cathleen* controversy shakes that support. Clearly such complexity makes Martyn a real-life figure.

16. Yeats's later formulation of himself (*A*, 307) as a heroic poseur could argue perhaps for his self-conscious awareness in adopting that pose. In any event, to adopt a meaningless, dated pose is still a futile unimaginative act.

17. George Moore in *Hail and Farewell* has accused the Yeats family of vulgar middle-class origin. He then went on to accuse Yeats of hypocrisy for his aristocratic condemnation of the middle-class Irish audience. To wipe out the possibility of any such analogous claim being made about the origins of his ideal family Yeats fabricates Lady Gregory's incredible heritage. Surely the unintended result is that later generations cannot take her as seriously as Yeats did for all his conscious fabrication.

18. All authority figures, of course, as seen by their dependents, are automatically objects of such ambivalent feelings.

19. See Elliot Jacques, "Death and the Mid-Life Crisis," *International Journal of Psycho-Analysis* (1965), 46:502–14.

20. The rest of the passage continues, pathetically: "I have reasoned myself out of the instincts and rules by which one mostly surrounds oneself. I have nothing but reason to trust to, and so am in continual doubt about simple things" (*A*, 273).

21. The particular formulation, "blindness and insight," is Paul de Man's. See his *Blindness and Insight: Essays in the Rhetoric of Contemporary Criticism* (New York: Oxford University Press, 1971). In essence, it means, as derived from Nietzsche and Heidegger, that the language of any particular interpretation often ironically reveals the most important insights in spite of the author's explicit intentions, insights to which because of his defensiveness or narrowness he must ever remain blind even as we are privileged to be his "seers." The phrase "innocence of becoming" is Kaufmann's translation of Nietzsche's term. See Nietzsche's *Twilight of the Idols* in *The Portable Nietzsche* (New York: Viking, 1954), pp. 499–500 and Kaufmann's *Nietzsche: Philosopher, Psychologist, Antichrist* (New York: Vintage, 1968), pp. 98, 166, 328, 330n., 375–76. Being able to allow oneself to become all the phases of that self one essentially must become if one is to be at all—without regrets, nostalgia, defensive cynicism, or *ressentiment*—this is the innocence of becoming. Primarily it refers not to the mercurial changes of the abstract modern ego, but rather to the necessary stages in the imaginative development of the creative self. See the subtitle of Nietzsche's own autobiography, *Ecce Homo*, for the most succinct formulation: "How One Becomes What One Is."

22. Though Yeats confesses to being a hopeless romantic in love at this time in his life (*A*, 289), he recalls his devotion to Maud Gonne with a bitterness still not assuaged by the distance of time: "My devotion might as well have been offered to an image in a milliner's window, or to a statue in a museum" (*A*, 267). Such bitterness explains Yeats's many detailed descriptions of Moore's abuse of the fairer sex much better than the simpler motive of objective criticism. For if that were Yeats's primary motive, one or two incidents would have sufficed.

23. See Ian Fletcher, "Rhythm and Pattern in 'Autobiographies,'" Denis Donoghue and J. R. Mulrayne, eds., *An Honoured Guest: New Essays on W. B. Yeats* (New York: St. Martin's Press, 1966), pp. 166 ff. Fletcher argues simply that Lady Gregory occupies these positions as part of Yeats's symbolic design of celebration. Though Moore receives the greatest bulk of his attention, she receives his most favorable emphasis. This is what Yeats consciously intends. But whether mere arrangement alone can make her become the ideal "centre of peace" for the volume is another matter.

24. *Collected Poems*, p. 187.

25. The modern creator, according to the rest of this passage, must fiercely analyze and compulsively test every word, since, in our time, the language and so ourselves have been spoiled by abstraction.

26. See Curtis Bradford, *"Autobiographies" and 'On the Boiler,' Yeats at Work* (Carbondale and Edwardsville: Southern Illinois University Press, 1965), pp. 338 ff.

27. I contend throughout that conscious use of the Mask (a concept also found in Nietzsche, *Beyond Good and Evil*, pp. 50–51), follows upon unconscious discovery, which itself follows in turn upon the conscious imposition of severely contrasting patterns of interpretation. The unconscious discovery, though provoked by the protracted conscious imposition of antithetical form, is always sudden, unpredictable, and truly a discovery rather than merely a final fulfillment of an intended program. This round of imposition and discovery makes up the peculiarly Yeatsian "hermeneutical circle" enacted in my interpretation.

28. Denis Donoghue in *William Butler Yeats* (New York: Viking, 1971) has made much of Nietzsche's influence on Yeats (primarily as the impetus to creative self-dramatization after the imaginative dead end of Pateresque stasis); and Patrick Keane has promised a definitive study of that influence. See *William Butler Yeats: A Collection of Critical Essays* (New York: McGraw-Hill, 1973). That Yeats read Nietzsche is clear from his letters and his library, and that he re-read and studied him from 1902 when John Quinn introduced him to Yeats until 1909–10 is equally clear from his many annotations of the passages in his copy of Thomas Common's anthology of Nietzsche's writings and those in his copies of Oscar Levy's edition of the complete works. Though this is not the place to delineate the exact nature and extent of Nietzsche's influence, I would like to suggest that it is definitive for any comprehensive understanding of Yeats's sudden blossoming into a major creator. See also Patrick Bridgewater, *Nietzsche in Anglosaxony* (Leicester: University of Leicester Press, 1972); and David S. Thatcher, *Nietzsche in England, 1890–1914: The Growth of a Reputation* (Toronto: University of Toronto Press, 1970).

29. These two figures are also Nietzsche's favorites. See Kaufmann, *Nietzsche*, p. 316. In fact, Nietzsche's ideal of the overman is the "Roman Caesar with Christ's soul" (*The Will to Power*, p. 513).

30. Though Yeats lists that egotism of the creator as one of the possible detractions from Synge's character, he does so clearly from the viewpoint of the world and not from that of the creative artist. In this way he can anticipate possible criticism of his own adoption of such an attitude.

31. See my first chapter for a further discussion.

32. The phrase is, of course, Nietzsche's. I mean it to refer to that central critical analysis of our culture that Yeats engages in at this time of his life under Nietzsche's influence.

33. See my first chapter. See also M. H. Abrams, *Natural Supernaturalism: Tradition and Revolution in Romantic Literature* (New York: Norton, 1971).

34. *Collected Poems*, "Three Movements," p. 236.

35. *Ibid.*, "The Tower," p. 195; "Nineteen Nineteen," p. 207.

36. Even the sentences are more paratactic. Where they are not they more often than not almost break into fragments, into notations: "I did not know that The Swedish Academy had ever heard my name; tried to escape an interview by talking of Rabindranath Tagore, of his gift to his School, of the seven thousand pounds awarded him; almost succeeded in dismissing the whole Reuter paragraph from my memory" (*A*, 358). A comic spirit marks both style and content here.

37. See *A*, 374–75 for an eighteen-line-long Yeatsian sentence which celebrates

the great Swedish Town Hall as the ideal combination of multiplicity and order, tradition and novelty, predetermined form and creative improvisation, all reminiscent of course of Byzantium at its height. Such idealizations are naturally important to the scholars of Yeats's opinions, and Joseph Ronsley in his study of *The Auto-biography* makes much of them. He even sees in them Yeats's approach to a symbolic vision of apocalypse. Such idealizations are important. For like Yeats's many-lined sentence describing the riches of the Gregory house (*A*, 260–61), they suggest that an indulgence in vision on Yeats's part invariably threatens his imaginative coherence. But they are simply not as important here, I would argue, as what happens to Yeats's own self-image of the creator.

38. Yeats chronically associates great feminine beauty with great artistic beauty—both seem the result of tremendous, even age-old creative labors. As such, beautiful women for him become the embodiment of his highest imaginative ideal. See the opening song of *The Only Jealousy of Emer, Collected Plays* (New York: Macmillan, 1973), p. 184:

> How many centuries spent
> The sedentary soul
> In toils of measurement
> Beyond eagle or mole,
> Beyond hearing or seeing,
> Or Archimedes's guess,
> To raise into being
> That loveliness?

39. The difference between tradition and conventions are perhaps too subtle for our modern tastes. In general, then, a tradition would be any body of belief that elicits our almost instinctual allegiance, whereas conventions would be customs self-consciously recognized as such, which one may or may not choose to comply with. That is, tradition reserves to itself all the vitality of the whole person, whereas convention requires only a formal and occasional intellectual assent. Thus, when a tradition of art sinks to the state of a convention, it means that its "world" is only believed in for purposes of executing a particular painting. It has become academic in every sense of the word. The artist's "fictions" are not mere conventions but compelling fragments of tradition repeatedly encountered.

40. *Collected Poems*, "High Talk," p. 331. This poem is a perfect comic counterpart for "Circus Animals' Desertion," p. 335. Whereas the latter poem may be accused of a grandiloquent, highly rhetorical turning to "the foul-rag-and-bone-shop of the heart," this poem admits all that and more: "All metaphor, Malachi, stilts and all." Here Yeats gets down off his ladder for real, and then mounts his metaphorical stilts for the fun of it. It is perhaps a healthier, though not as obviously "important" poem.

41. *Collected Poems*, "Vacillation," p. 246.

42. *Ibid.*, "Lapis Lazuli," p. 292.

4. THE FALTERING IMAGE

43. Friedrich Nietzsche, *On the Genealogy of Morals*, pp. 99.

44. See Alan Wilde, *Christopher Isherwood* (New York: Twayne, 1971), pp. 14–26, for an excellent analysis of the final development of irony into an autonomous vision expressive of a bitter alienation from existence that defines early modernism. See also "Depths and Surfaces: Some Aspects of Forsterian Irony," *ELT* (Fall 1973), 15:1–16.

45. Paul de Man, "Genesis and Genealogy in Nietzsche's *The Birth of Tragedy*," *Diacritics* (Winter 1972), pp. 44–53, and "Nietzsche's Theory of Rhetoric," *Symposium* (Spring 1974), pp. 33–51, see especially p. 47.

46. Søren Kierkegaard, *The Concept of Irony with Constant Reference to Socrates*, Lee Capel, trans. (Bloomington and London: Indiana University Press, 1971), pp. 336–42 (on "mastered irony") and pp. 132–33 (on irony's relation to the mythical).

47. Friedrich Nietzsche, *The Birth of Tragedy*, Francis Goffling, trans. (Garden City: Doubleday, 1956), from the "Preface," p. 15.

48. See Alan Wilde, *Art and Order: A Study of E. M. Forster* (New York: New York University Press, 1964), pp. 16–26, for a full description of what he terms "the aesthetic view of life," a view Joyce captures brilliantly in his portrait of Stephen Dedalus.

49. *Collected Poems*, "Nineteen Nineteen," p. 206.

50. *Ibid.*, "Under Ben Bulben," p. 342.

51. Hugh Kenner, "The Sacred Book of the Arts," in John Unterrecker ed., *Yeats: A Collection of Critical Essays* (Englewood Cliffs, N.J.: Prentice-Hall, 1963), pp. 10–22; J. Hillis Miller, *Poets of Reality* (New York: Antheneum, 1965), pp. 68–130.

52. Nietzsche, *On the Genealogy of Morals*, pp. 77–78. This notion of the tradition of interpretation as a species of creative adaptation to the conditions of life is extremely suggestive for a more fruitful understanding of literacy history than that provided by either Eliot's or Bloom's notions.

53. Nietzsche, *Ecce Homo* (included in the same volume as *On the Genealogy of Morals*), p. 258.

54. *Collected Poems*, "A Dialogue of Self and Soul," p. 232. It is usually said that the poem ends with the Self having the last word, as if the Soul and its arguments were simply forgotten. But as these lines show this is simply not the case. Instead, after the Self admits the Soul's antithetical role in the formation of Yeats's hopeless love for Maud Gonne, he then emphasizes that when he casts out remorse the result is that both Self and Soul can be reunited in the blessed dance of the creator's eternal return of all Yeats's temporal perspectives no matter how painful, no matter how joyous. Soul and Self become whole for a brief moment here at the site of the text thanks to Yeats's will-to-power over himself, his self-overcoming.

Index

Abrams, M. H. 14, 16, 30, 47, 164n7, 185n33; romantic paradigm of autobiography, 9–12
Ascendency, 4–5, 115, 121
Autobiographical theory, 10–16

Bedford Park, 27; as Pre-Raphaelite experiment, 81–83
Blake, William, 25; as influence on Yeats in shaping *Reveries*, 77–80
Bloom, Harold, 34, 163n3, 166n21, 167n31, 168n44, 171n28, 181n4; on revisionism, 9; on Yeats's gnosticism, 17, 50; on *Autobiography*, 17, 164n3,
Bové, Paul A., 165n15, 168n44, 170n73

Chatterjee, Mohini, 73, 74
Coleridge, Samuel Taylor, 176n8
Conrad, Joseph, 182n7
Coole Park, 107, 120–21

Daimon, 112–13, 141, 144; as romantic image of poet, 5; as Yeats's creator-figure, 25, 29, 45, 49; Shelley's influence on Yeats's conception, 88–92; Nietzsche's influence, 97; Wilde as victim of his daimon, 99–102; Yeats's central symbol for, 103–6; Yeats's later ironic version of, 136–42; recent critical commentary on, 168n43; relation to Arnold's "buried self" and Jung's "god-image," 175n7

Dancer, 106–7
Davidson, John, 103, 104; ironic inspiration for vision, 105–6
Deconstruction, 4, 33, 34, 35, 136–38; relation to autobiographical theory, 11–13; Yeats's deconstructive practice in *Autobiography* (summary), 136–40
de Man, Paul, 44, 182n7; as theorist of autobiography, 9–12
Derrida, Jacques, 42, 44; on 'play', 174n3
Dionysus, 19, 46
Donato, Eugenio, 13; on Hegel's continuing influence on critics, 165n14
Dowden, Edward, 72, 73; Yeats's intentionally distorted image of, 177n12

Eliot, T. S., 9, 13, 164n6
Ellmann, Richard, 18, 171n8; Yeats's 'affirmative capability', 182n7

Farr, Florence, 83; ruined mind as representative of 'Tragic Generation', 175n4
Fiction, 182n7
Fletcher, Ian, 19, 166n29; as critic of *Autobiography*, 17–18

Gadamer, Hans Georg, 34, 42; his philosophical hermeneutics, 39
Goethe, 1, 175n6

Gonne, Maud, 20, 83, 84; as tragic symbol of Yeats's art, 108–9
Gregory, Lady Augusta, 18, 53, 107, 183*n*11, 17; as symbolic mother figure for Yeats, 122–23

Hegel, G. W. F., 2, 9, 165*n*15, 165*n*17; as theorist of 'tragic knowledge', 12–16; relation to Ricoeur, 19, 30, 35; relation to Yeats's autobiographical project 50; continuing influence on contemporary critics, 165*n*14
Heidegger, Martin, 2; 'destructive hermeneutics', 14, 37, 169*n*62; critique by Ricoeur, 41–43; influence on de Man, 181–82*n*6
Hermeneutics: hermeneutic circle, 3; temporal nature, 4; historical horizons, 13; dialectical form, 17, 30, 33, 35, 36, 38–39; as applied to irony, 30
Hoy, David Couzzens: on Hegel and Heidegger, 13, 165*n*14, 169*n*64; on hermeneutic circle, 163*n*4

Ihde, Don, 169*n*52
Irony: as typically represented in autobiography, 1, 8; theory of, 11–13; 170*n*2; 182–83*n*8; Yeats's daimonic conception of, 17, 18, 23, 28, 30–32; as organizing principle in *Autobiography*, 117–21, 133–36, 150–54

Jacques, Elliott, 184*n*19
Johnson, Lionel, 18, 177*n*1; as tragic symbol of poetic craftsman, 105
Jung, C. G., 2; on 'god-image', 13, 168*n*42, 175*n*5, 175*n*7; on 'temenos spot', 178*n*16, 180*n*29

Kaufmann, Walter, 164*n*2; on Nietzsche's dialectic, 186*n*29
Keane, Patrick, 166*n*24

Kenner, Hugh, 181*n*51; on Yeats's ironic rhetoric, 15, 158, 166*n*27
Kermode, Frank, 18, 166*n*28; on Yeats's use of romantic image of dancer, 178*n*21
Kierkegaard, Søren, 14, 136–37, 187*n*46; on irony, 136–37 on repetition, 179*n*26
Kohut, Hans, 166*n*24

Life-crisis, 184*n*9
Lynch, David: on failure of *Autobiography*, 17, 18; on daimonic in Yeats, 166*n*24

Mallarmé, Stephan, 177*n*14, 180*n*33
Martyn, Edward, 181*n*5; as Moore's 'saintly' counterpart, 116–17
Mask: as self-creation, 2, 5; relation to 'play', 8; Yeats's idea of, 17, 18, 19–20, 23, 28–29, 48–51, 84–86, 88–92, 168*n*43; relation to Ricoeur's hermeneutics, 34–35; relation to Nietzsche's irony 39–40; as sign of 'tragic knowledge', 45–46, 185*n*27
Mathers, Macgregor, 26, 102; influence of his art of meditation on Yeats, 27–28
Mehlman, Jeffrey, 164*n*11; his autobiographical theory as witty reversal of tradition, 13
Misch, Georg, 164*n*11; traditional definition of autobiography as a genre, 13
Moore, George, 21, 181*n*5, 184*n*22; as Yeats's ironic nemesis, 123–25; as Yeats's collaborator, 183*n*13; his relations with Lady Gregory, 183*n*17
Morris, William, 86–88
Muecke, D. C.; on 'philosophical irony', 182–83*n*8
Murphy, William; *Prodigal Father*, 167*n*35

Nietzsche, Friedrich, 1, 2; *Of the Use and Disadvantage of History for Life,* xii; *Ecce Homo,* 3, 115, 187*n*53; *Thus Spoke Zarathustra,* 4, 7; *Will to Power,* 7–8, 9, 53, 163*n*1, 179*n*24; and self-invention, 8, 15, 20, 21, 23, 164*n*2; on 'tragic knowledge', 25, 29, 45, 46, 170*n*72; *Schopenhauer as Educator,* 39–40; on self-knowledge, 40, 50; *Birth of Tragedy,* 45, 170*n*72; relation to Yeats's daimonic irony, 97, 133–36, 137–40, 142–44, 168*n*47, 182–83*n*7; *Genealogy of Morals,* 115, 148, 150, 187*n*43, 187*n*52; on ideas as 'fictions', 179*n*24; *Beyond Good And Evil,* 185*n*27; studies of influence on Yeats, 185*n*28; and dialectical art, 186*n*29

O'Grady, Standish, 131–32
O'Leary, 77, 173*n*19, 177*n*10; as Yeats's early image of hero, 75–76
Olney, James, 13, 19, 164*n*12, 167*n*31

Palmer, Richard, 166*n*20
Parnel, Charles Stewart, 176*n*9, 177*n*11
Pascal, Roy, 164*n*4
Pater, Walter, 50; as influence on 'tragic generation', 109–11
Perloff, Majorie, 17, 19; theoretical naiveté, 171*n*1, 173*n*1
Phantasmagoria, 28, 95–97
'Play', 8, 42, 44, 113, 174*n*3
Poéte Maudit, 17, 18, 99–102; Oscar Wilde as Yeats's model, 86–88
Pollexfen, George, 71–72
Pollexfen, William, 55, 59, 60; as Yeats's initial antithetical symbol in *Autobiography,* 56–58

Quinn, John, 20, 185*n*28

Reid, B. L., 166*n*17
Revisionsim, 7–9

Ricoeur, Paul, 1, 2, 33, 38, 41–44; dialectic of reference and self-reference, 9, 12; dialectical hermeneutics, 16–17, 33–46; relation to Hegel, 34–35; "From Existentialism to Philosophy of Language," 35, 169*n*53; *Symbolism of Evil,* 35; *Freud and Philosophy,* 35, 37; early idea of symbol, 37; *Interpretation Theory,* 37, 39, 40–41, 169*n*51; idea of metaphor, 37, 44; *Rule of Metaphor,* 37, 44, 163*n*2, 168*n*50; definitive theory of interpretation, 37–39; usefulness for reading autobiography, 39–41; critique of Heidegger, 41–43; use of Gadamer, 41; return to Aristotle's conception of poet, 43; on tragic awareness, 50, 53; *History and Truth,* 50, 53, 170*n*74; summary of role in understanding *Autobiography,* 158–61; "Fatherhood: From Phantasm to Symbol," 167*n*40; "The Task of Hermeneutics," 169*n*54; "What Is a Text?", 172*n*16
Ronsley, Joseph, 17, 19, 166*n*17, 26
Russell, George (A. E.), 24, 25, 26; Yeats's antithetical relation with, 93–95

Said, Edward, 168*n*48
Schlegel, Friedrich, 163*n*15
Schopenhauer, Arthur, 8, 15; as Nietzsche's 'sublime' educator, 39–40
Shelley, Percy Bysshe, 22, 50, 167*n*41; his *Hellas* as source for Yeats's figure of wise creator or sage, 88–92
Socrates, 5, 15
Spanos, William V., 169*n*63; polemic against New Critics, 163*n*5, 180*n*32
Spengemann, William C, 165*n*72
Sprinker, Michael, 13
Stockholm, 146; Yeats's complex impressions of, 147–48

191

Style, 133–36
Symbol, 37; views of Goethe and
  Coleridge, 175n6
Synge, John Millington, 133–36,
  180n28; Yeats on aristocratic style of
  his self-victimage, 133, 136

Taylor, John F., 75; as rhetorician and
  O'Leary's foil, 76–77
Thatcher, David S., 168n47, 185n78
Tragic knowledge: as daimonic form of
  irony, 1, 2, 4–5; as represented in
  autobiographical writing, 7–9;
  Hegelian idea of, 14–16; Yeatsian
  vision of, 25, 29, 32, 47–48; relation
  to Ricoeur's interpretation theory,
  37–38; Nietzsche's revision, 39–40,
  45–46, 170n72; as defined in Yeats's
  autobiographical writings, 51; as
  produced in Yeats's *Autobiography*,
  77–80, 97–98, 109–11, 148–150,
  151–54
Tynan, Katharine, 21

Whittaker, Thomas R., 166n17
Wilde, Alan: *Horizons of Assent*,
  170n72, 182–83n8; *Art and Order*,
  187n48; *Christopher Isherwood*, 187n44
Wilde, Oscar, 13, 18, 24, 86–88; as
  Yeats's model of *poéte maudit*, 99–102

Yeats, J. B., 63–68; opinion of
  Nietzsche's influence on his son,
  167n35
Yeats, William Butler, 2, 3, 4, 17–33,
  46–51; Nietzschean pose, 5, 16, 21,
  29, 97, 167n35, 182–83n8, 183n9,
  185n28; on irony, 17, 20–21, 34;

relation to Nietzsche and Pater on
  Greeks, 23; antithetical method of
  self-interpretation, 25–26, 41; idea of
  'tragic knowledge', 25, 29, 32, 47–48;
  on anti-self as daimonic creator,
  28–29, 46, 48; ironic self-dedication
  to art, 30–31, 68–70; modern
  revision of Blakean vision of
  childhood, 77–80; symbolic dialectic,
  84–86; major autobiographical
  symbols, 86–88; origins, 88–92;
  central symbol of creator, 103–6;
  Unity of Being and Dancer image
  revised, 106–7; Maud Gonne as
  symbol of his art, 108–9; on Pater's
  aesthetic philosophy, 109–11; his
  gnostic tendencies, 111–13,
  180–81n39; daimonic meditations on
  style, 133–36; deconstruction of
  romantic image of poet, 136–40; his
  'affirmative capability', 182n7
—— *works:* "Among School Children,"
  44; *A Vision*, 15, 16; *Autobiography*,
  critics of, 17–19; title changes, 164n5;
  "Dialogue of Self and Soul," 161;
  Dramatis Personae, as revision of
  romantic form of genre, 141–44,
  150–54; "Ego Dominus Tuus," 48,
  92; "First Principles," 22–23; "High
  Talk," 115, 148; *Only Jealousy of
  Emer*, 109, 186n38; "Pardon Old
  Fathers," 20; analyzed, 20–21;
  "Poetry and Tradition," 32–34; "A
  Prayer for My Daughter," 113;
  Reveries, as ironic modern version of
  Blake's vision of childhood, 77–80;
  Trembling of the Veil, as self-mocking
  'play' to summon daimon, 111–13;
  "Vacillation," 51, 163n7